spring 2017

Mission

We understand "community literacy" as the domain for literacy work that exists outside of conventional educational and work institutions. It can be found in programs devoted to adult education, early childhood education, reading initiatives, lifelong learning, workplace literacy, or work with marginalized populations, but it can also be found in more informal, ad hoc projects.

For us, literacy is defined as the realm where attention is paid not just to content or to knowledge but to the symbolic means by which it is represented and used. Thus, literacy makes reference not just to letters and to text but to other multimodal and technological representations as well. We publish work that contributes to the field's emerging methodologies and research agendas.

Subscriptions

As of January 1st, 2016, the *CLJ* will no longer offer subscriptions to individuals. It will now accept donations to support continuing publication.

Donations to the *CLJ* in any amount can be made with:
- a credit card at http://bit.ly/2jjn5ig
- a check made out to "UA Foundation," with the *Community Literacy Journal* in the memo line.

Send checks to:
John Warnock
Department of English
University of Arizona
Tucson, AZ 85721

Donors at the $50 level or above will be sent print copies of the academic year's issues as a gift and given electronic access to the *CLJ*'s present and past issues, upon request to John Warnock at the mailing address above or at johnw@email.arizona.edu.

The *CLJ* is a 501(c)(3) organization. Donations to the *CLJ* may be tax deductible.

Cover Art

Photograph: paz y amor por vida: consejos de south tucson (arte urbano series)
by Adela C. Licona

adela c. licona's photography captures surface and depth. with camera in hand, she studies facets, textures, colors, patterns, & forms at times to document and at times to interrogate the mundane. she approaches her object photography as well as her eco-scapes, arte urbano/ city-scapes, and body-scapes as "assemblages of stories so far." through a developed intensity in focus, her photographs often invite deeper inspections of the everyday. as artist, scholar, & public rhetor, she is interested in provoking & participating in new ways of seeing & looking — reorientations, meaningful distortions, & re/visionings that are informed by — and might also inform — radical re/imaginings of being, belonging, and relating to one another, to everyday objects & everyday-scapes, to histories & bodies, to places & practices, and to the earth. especially now. in 2017. eyes, hearts, and minds wide open. you can follow adela on instagram @entremundista

Submissions

The peer-reviewed *Community Literacy Journal* seeks contributions for upcoming issues. We welcome submissions that address social, cultural, rhetorical, or institutional aspects of community literacy; we particularly welcome pieces authored in collaboration with community partners.

Manuscripts should be submitted according to the standards of the *MLA Handbook for Writers of Research Papers*, 7th ed. (New York: MLA).

Shorter and longer pieces are acceptable (8–25 manuscript pages) depending on authors' approaches. Case studies, reflective pieces, scholarly articles, etc., are all welcome.

To submit manuscripts, visit our site—communityliteracy.org—and register as an author. Send queries to Michael Moore: mmoore46@depaul.edu.

Advertising

The *Community Literacy Journal* welcomes advertising. The journal is published twice annually, in the Fall and Spring (Nov. and Mar.). Deadlines for advertising are two months prior to publication (Sept. and Jan.).

Ad Sizes and Pricing

Half page (trim size 6x4.5)	$200
Full page (trim size 6x9)	$350
Inside back cover (trim size 6x9)	$500
Inside front cover (trim size 6x9)	$600

Format

We accept .PDF, .JPG, .TIF or .EPS. All advertising images should be camera-ready and have a minimum resolution of 300 DPI. For more information, please contact Michael Moore: mmoore46@depaul.edu.

Copyright © 2017 *Community Literacy Journal*
ISSN 1555-9734

The *Community Literacy Journal* is a member of the Council of Editors of Learned Journals Printing and distribution managed by Parlor Press.

Editorial Advisory Board

Jonathan Alexander	University of California, Irvine
Nancy Guerra Barron	Northern Arizona University
David Barton	Lancaster University, UK
David Blakesley	Clemson University
Melody Bowdon	University of Central Florida
Tara Brabazon	Flinders University, Australia
Danika Burgess	Rice University
Ernesto Cardenal	Casa de los Tres Mundos, Managua
Marilyn Cooper	Michigan Technological University
Linda Flower	Carnegie Mellon University
Diana George	Virginia Tech University
Jeff Grabill	Michigan State University
Laurie Grobman	Pennsylvania State University
Greg Hart	YWCA Southern Arizona
Shirley Brice Heath	Stanford University
Tobi Jacobi	Colorado State University
Lou Johnson	River Parishes YMCA, New Orleans
Paula Mathieu	Boston College
Regina Mokgokong	Project Literacy, Pretoria, South Africa
Ruth E. Ray	Wayne State University
Georgia Rhoades	Appalachian State University
Mike Rose	University of California, Los Angeles
Lauren Rosenberg	New Mexico State University
Tiffany Rousculp	Salt Lake Community College
Cynthia Selfe	The Ohio State University
Tanya Shuy	U.S. Department of Education
Vanderlei de Souza	Faculdade de Tecnologia de Carapicuíba, São Paulo
John Trimbur	Emerson College
Christopher Wilkey	Northern Kentucky University

COMMUNITY LITERACY *journal*

Editors Michael R. Moore
DePaul University

John Warnock
University of Arizona

Senior Assistant Editor Amanda Gaddam
DePaul University

Assistant Editors Mariana Grohowski
Indiana University Southeast

Design & Production Editor Ekram Othman
DePaul University

Copy Editors Saul Hernandez
Georgia College and State University

Sarah Hughes
Washtenaw Community College

Dana Jabri
DePaul University

Katelyn Pfaff
DePaul University

Bridget Wagner
DePaul University

Kelly Whitney
New Mexico State University

COMMUNITY LITERACY Journal

Journal Manager Mike Hernandez
DePaul University

Book & New Media Review Editor Jessica Shumake
University of Arizona

Saul Hernandez, Assistant Editor
Georgia College and State University

Social Media Editor Janel R. G. Murakami
University of Arizona

Consulting Editors Rachel Buck
University of Arizona

Maria Conti
University of Arizona

Janel R. G. Murakami
University of Arizona

Eric Plattner
DePaul University

Stephanie Vie
University of Central Florida

community literacy journal

COMMUNITY LITERACY journal

Spring 2017
Volume 11 Issue 2

Articles

1   Brokering Literacies:
Child Language Brokering in Mexican Immigrant Families
Steven Alvarez

16   "My Little English":
a Case Study of Decolonial Perspectives on Discourse
in an After-School Program for Refugee Youth
Michael T. MacDonald

30   Looking Outward:
Archival Research as Community Engagement
Whitney Douglas

43   Who Researches Functional Literacy?
Donita Shaw, Kristen H. Perry, Lyudmyla Ivanyuk, Sarah Tham

65   Navigating Difficulty in Classroom-Community Outreach Projects
Lauren Rosenberg

Book & New Media Reviews

74 From the Book & New Media Review Editor's Desk
Jessica Shumake
Saul Hernandez, Assistant Editor

76 Reframing the Subject:
Postwar Instructional Film and Class-Conscious Literacies
By Kelly Ritter
Reviewed by Christopher M. Brown

80 The Slow Professor:
Challenging the Culture of Speed in the Academy
By Maggie Berg and Barbara K. Seeber
Reviewed by Sandra D. Shattuck

84 Composition in the Age of Austerity
Edited by Nancy Welch and Tony Scott
Reviewed by Rachel Buck

89 Grassroots Literacies:
Lesbian and Gay Activism and the Internet in Turkey
By Serkan Görkemli
Reviewed by Madelyn Pawlowski

93 The Desire for Literacy:
Writing in the Lives of Adult Learners
By Lauren Rosenberg
Reviewed by Sally Benson

98 Freedom Writing:
African American Civil Rights Literacy Activism, 1955–1967
By Rhea Estelle Lathan
Reviewed by Eric A. House

Brokering Literacies:
Child Language Brokering in Mexican Immigrant Families

Steven Alvarez

Abstract

This article reports from instances of child language brokering among emergent bilingual youths and parents at a New York City after-school community literacy program composed largely of Mexican immigrant families. I argue that youth language brokers negotiated literacies with and for their parents in differing contexts, with different audiences, and under different dynamics of power relations. Young language brokers utilize bilingual practices to translate, interpret, and advise between adults and family members of different ages. Language brokers, I argue, use their bilingual learning to help their families and to show they care.

Keywords: language brokering, bilingual learning, immigrant families, family literacies

This article reports on five years of ethnographic research into the day-to-day instances of child language brokering among emergent bilingual youths and parents at a New York City after-school community literacy program composed largely of Mexican immigrant families. My research explores the languages and literacies of participant bilingual youth language brokers, bilingual mediators who communicate between monolingual adults. These youth language brokers negotiated meaning with and for their parents in differing contexts, with different audiences, and under different dynamics of power relations. The young language brokers utilized varying levels of bilingual practices to effectively increase translate, interpret, and advise between adults and family members of different ages. Bilingual brokers develop practices to navigate complex information in their family lives, which would never be fully evaluated in their schooling, but yet which schools would seem to expect or even demand in terms of family-involved literacy learning among "gifted" students (Valdés).

My research examines language brokering among mothers and children and the day-to-day literacy practices of children participating in the Mexican American Network of Students (MANOS) community literacy after-school program. The

MANOS language brokers involved and engaged monolingual Spanish dominant family members in their schooling lives, which were largely conducted in English. This positive aspect of language brokering, however, balanced with power differences that happen in bilingual exchanges. Language brokering collaborations sometimes produce conflicts from linguistic inequalities, which re-distribute intergenerational authority between parents and children. Depending on the contexts, being aware of these power differences can also be places for literacy researchers to recognize how bilingual parental collaborations with children happen in families. This last aspect adds to the learning of emergent bilingual students who come to understand the responsibilities of language brokers when communicating with diverse audiences, including educators.

Research in language brokering has examined the complex strategies of youth language brokers navigating audiences, languages, and literacies (Orellana; Orellana and García; Orellana and Reynolds; Orellana et al.; Weisskirch). This article adds to a line of ethnographic research into language brokering as saturated with conflicting authorities and social bridges between languages and cultures. As in previous research portraying children as social actors living in their existential present, and not as "adults in the making" (Corsaro 225), I speak directly with youth language brokers to consider how young people's understandings of their families, their educations, and their languages actively contribute to each as they see themselves in their everyday lives. In this article, the social values of non-standard, minoritized languages and literacy practices demonstrate how two youths felt about language brokering and its power in their families, particularly when translating to help their mothers in different contexts.

Language brokers occupy a unique position in communication. In *Translating Childhoods: Immigrant Youth, Language, and Culture*, Marjorie Faulstich Orellana argues that youth language brokers mediate adult-to-adult conversations and often voice their concerns about the translated contents of both oral and written texts between different monolingual audiences. The MANOS children brokered for mothers around the neighborhood, but also in such tense circumstances as admission to emergency rooms, and interviews with counselors and lawyers. In one case, Sarita, the 17-year-old daughter of 38-year-old Guadalupe, brokered between her Spanish-speaking mother and the English-speaking teachers of her two younger brothers (in fourth and first grade), offering her mother more than mere translations; she provided Guadalupe analyses of situations and assumed the function of adviser when six-year-old Miguel was diagnosed with a speech impediment and required therapy appointments. Especially in matters relating to school and guarding her younger brothers, Sarita's bilingual abilities to shuttle across languages had increased her family stature in the eyes of Guadalupe. This sense of "role reversal" could misguidedly be seen as a result of when children socialize their parents, or become parents for their children. To understand such power dynamics in a more nuanced way, however, we must consider how language brokering becomes a way that children help their parents as a form of respect and familial duty.

To understand the potential social and academic benefits language brokering might have for children, we must also understand how translation functions beyond language and literacy into the lives of families. As Orellana contends, second-generation language brokers in families do not always see themselves as parents to their parents. Rather, language broker youth consider their translations and interpretations as contributions to the good of the family, as a way of demonstrating care. Young people help their family members with their language brokering, and in doing so, they enact social relationships between audiences. Language brokers meet where English and Spanish circulate and conflict in overlapping markets of cultural values, histories, and power. Language brokers are attuned in to this awareness in their day-to-day linguistic interactions, especially as they not only translate and interpret, but they often advise as well. These aspects of language brokering are important for educators to recognize, and they demonstrate the powerful tools that young language brokers utilize on a daily basis. As such, pedagogy inclusive to this feature of the home lives of millions of students underscores overlooked cultural, intellectual and linguistic strengths language brokers bring to classrooms across the nation.

Study Context: MANOS, the Mexican American Network of Students

This article draws from a larger research project into how English language acquisition and literacy transformed family relations and structured educational ambitions among tutors and MANOS families. Nine first-generation Mexican-origin immigrant families (9 mothers, 21 children) living in New York City were the focus of my study, all members of MANOS, a small, underfunded, self-sustained community literacy program, whose core of dedicated volunteers were also participants in this qualitative study. The grassroots MANOS offered free evening homework tutoring services three times a week, Mondays, Tuesdays, and Fridays. MANOS promoted active family involvement in schooling and positive views toward ethnolinguistic identity. The MANOS tutors varied in ages from 16 to late 50s. The majority, however, were young professionals in their twenties who volunteered once or twice a week, some all three evenings. Several tutors arrived to the program in their office clothes, and a few came from distant parts of other boroughs. Nearly all the tutors were second-generation Mexican Americans and first-generation college students. Several tutors were from different regions of the United States attending college in New York City. There was also a steady stream of local high school students and international university students from Mexico City who volunteered as tutors while earning community service hours to meet graduation requirements. All tutors spoke and wrote English, and some were more fluent in Spanish than others. For one tutor, Mandarin was her first language, Spanish her second, and English her third. Tutors who had the capacities to use Spanish when communicating with MANOS families did so. Children of parents also helped with language brokering duties to parents and young children who had little comprehension of English.

MANOS's mothers were the program's most important assets. In *Mexican New York: Transnational Lives of New Immigrants*, Robert C. Smith argues that gender roles in the Mexican family division of labor point to the cultural responsibility of education as within "female" spaces (97). By and large, the participation among children and tutors fell evenly between females and males, but among parents, there were more participant mothers than fathers at MANOS. At different times fathers also helped with homework, fundraising, and maintaining the space. By tutoring at MANOS, though, I learned about families through the interactions I had with mothers and children, as mothers were the primary regular caretakers I encountered. The MANOS mothers were exceptional in helping their children succeed in school, and they contributed to their children's educational needs in manners deemed fit and necessary for their children's well-being.

The data for my project was gathered primarily over a period of five years, beginning in early 2006, when I conducted my first round of family interviews in homes and at MANOS. These interviews were conducted in both Spanish and English with bilingual children and/or tutors serving as language brokers when possible. I digitally audio-recorded these interviews, as well as interactions with parents, children, and myself when working through homework, or when speaking, writing and/or reading at the MANOS center. Data consisted of digitally recaptured images of texts produced by MANOS children, parents, and tutors, photographs, as well as transcripts from interviews and tutoring sessions.

Using methods developed from my reading of Shirley Brice Heath's *Ways with Words: Language, Life and Work in Communities in Classrooms*, I initially coded audio-recorded homework tutorials involving tutors, parents, and children into different examples of language brokering as literacy events, searching for moments of translation as data for literacy as social practice. When examining instances of language brokering through the data, I problematized Heath's notions of literacy events as limited to monolingual conceptions of literacy brokering. I reconfigured, instead, literacy events in plurilingual dimensions, and in more recent research I have considered them as moments of "translanguaging events" reflecting the dynamic practices of individuals in bilingual contexts (Alvarez 326). In this article, I focus on such translanguaging events narrated as a vignette of a young person helping his mother during an exchange, and the reflection of another student when considering his history of language brokering for his mother as a form of family duty.

MANOS Serving Mexicanos in New York

The majority of my fieldwork occurred at the MANOS site, in the basement of a Catholic Church in one of New York City's outer boroughs, a space the church donated to MANOS for six hours each week. Historically, the neighborhood had been home to immigrant groups since the early nineteenth century. According to the Latino Data Project at the Graduate Center of the City of New York, in 2010, Mexicans composed 14.3% of New York City's total Latino population, with a growth rate of nearly 10% between 1990-2010 (4). At the time of this study, the neighborhood was one of New York City's "Little Mexico" immigrant barrios. Like several barrios in New York City, the Mexican community initially concentrated in the middle of a predominantly Puerto Rican neighborhood. Because of the racial diversity of New York City, the boroughs' "Little Mexicos" were often ethnically and racially diverse, and they have emerged around areas with relatively recent Spanish-speaking migrants from Latin America.

The growth of New York City's Mexican immigrant community underscores the need for MANOS's services to the neighborhood. Yet, despite an enormous unmet need for educational services, MANOS struggled to continue because of lack of institutional support. The underfunded, grassroots organization had struggled year by year to secure a donated location, to recruit tutors, to pay for heat during the winters, and, generally, to provide sufficient services to its members. Despite these hardships, MANOS had persevered for nearly a decade through the sheer will of its volunteer tutors and its member families. Though MANOS remained essentially a small-scale, family-driven after-school program, a long-standing goal had continually been to change its shape through its leadership and achieving legitimate non-profit 501(c)(3) status. This goal had been seen as a work-in-progress. Although less structured than most funded after-school programs, among the numerous social organizations mobilized by Mexican immigrants in New York City, MANOS was recognized as an established program and had won several honors from New York City and State governments, as well as from various cultural organizations in the tristate area, for its services to New York's Mexican community.

Language Brokering: Linguistic Power in Families

The linguistic activities of brokering and being brokers tint all the exchanges of languages analyzed in this study. To language broker is to serve as liaison with influence in exchanges between individuals, to partake in an exchange as an active audience assuming creative or independent agency. According to Lucy Tse, language brokers "influence the content and nature of the message they convey, and ultimately affect the perceptions and decisions of the agents for whom they act" (180). Robert S. Weisskirch argues that during language brokering, "the authority position of the parent may be suppressed as the child or adolescent acts as the spokesperson for the family" (546). During such cases, Carola Suárez-Orozco and Marcelo M. Suárez-Orozco claim that children of immigrants can become "parentified" (74–5). Maria Elena Puig also terms this possibility of role reversal of children and parents as "adultification" in her sample of Cuban refugee families (85).

Without doubt, there were are instances when language brokering disrupts power dynamics among parents and children, but these repositionings are not stable, as no child wields consistent power over parents. How the relations fluctuate is only a matter of contexts and situations. Power reversals are both positive and negative effects of language brokering, but bilingual practices develop in the movement between languages in communication. When the MANOS youths assisted their parents with written and spoken English, there sometimes indeed was a family role reversal where children socialized parents through language brokering, but less in a way to treat their parents as children. When I asked different MANOS youths about translating for their parents, they described language brokering as something they owed their parents, on a level with keeping spaces clean and doing homework.

Several of the MANOS youths had reported to me they were sometimes precociously pushed by their translation responsibilities to assume adult-like authority in their families for the making of meaning and choices, especially when dealing in official genres like applications, disciplinary reports, parent notices, and school permission slips. The linguistic power these bilingual youths cultivated happened as they were compelled to grow up prematurely through translating both meanings and consequences of such official texts. Lisa M. Dorner et al. argue that "children take on a wide variety of translating tasks and that these require considerable linguistic, arithmetic, and social-cultural dexterity" (452). The researchers provide examples of bilingual youth who "explain their own or siblings' report cards to their parents, translate at doctor's offices and banks, make purchases at local drug stores, fill out credit card applications, screen phone calls from telemarketers, and translate movies and television shows for family and friends" (452). Added to this dimension of family responsibility, the sociocultural practices of language brokering are the extension into bilingualism as a valuable aspect of family life for immigrants. Without a doubt, this "parentified" sense of power happened through the reinforcement of the linguistic marketplace and the exchange value behind the acquisition of the dominant language. But the rewards of language brokering could also be redistributed to the family for its communal good. The scholars who argue that language brokering complicates parent-child protocols in immigrant families must take note that language brokering is not the sole cause of the breakdown of communication or language loss in immigrant families. Language brokering is a day-to-day activity, and it deserves pedagogical appreciation. Language brokering can be a tool to reach the literacies of families and to increase involvement and interest in language learning.

One possibility to approaching this as a pedagogical opportunity is to affirm the positive attributes recognizing children's voices, their "adultification," or by affirming the positive attributes of children's linguistic power, and giving greater appreciation to these skills in curricula. Lucy Tse reports that the Latino students in her sample described mixed positive and negative emotions with regards to their brokering, ranging from embarrassed and burdened to proud, independent, and mature (192). Marjorie Faulstich Orellana reports that adolescents in her studies demonstrated feelings of responsibility and power in their roles as language brokers for their parents (57). Curtis J. Jones and Edison J. Trickett recognize the potential value for the social act of brokering in immigrant families. Translating for their parents, they claim, indeed may prove stressful for youth, but that "such activities may, in principle, also be a source of family solidarity and an opportunity to increase self-efficacy and sense of importance" (409). MANOS youths also reported that serving as a language broker for their parents was a tedious, sometimes embarrassing event, but that it was also something useful to help their families.

Brokering English and Authority: Language Brokering and Family Duties
Increasingly, my fieldwork at MANOS revealed to me how immigrant parents who attended the grassroots community literacy program gave great weight to their

language brokering children's advice in normatively parental domains of family life. This was when situations become both moments for learning and also for questioning the influence of children in immigrant families, both as a situation for power disruption and also for acquisition of language skills. The shifts of power between generations I found, however, happened less intensely than as presented in language brokering and literacy research. This, however, did not mean that children were completely ruled by their parents, or that they ruled their parents, but, rather, they took pride in the power their English commanded, especially when they were able to use it to help their parents. Eleven-year-old Felipe Rubio (brother of Sarita, mentioned earlier) described a recent memory when he language brokered for his mother, 38-year-old Guadalupe,

> Like we went to a store and it's only me and my mom, and we talked to someone who didn't speak Spanish. And I said what they said to my mom, and I told the other person what my mom said, and helped both of the people. It made me feel like I know more Spanish. It felt like . . . like I helped my mom with something. It makes me feel proud, because I'm doing a good thing. I'm doing something good.

Felipe's language brokering completed the shopping transaction, and for Felipe, his involvement with adults made him feel like he knew more Spanish, or that he was putting his Spanish skills to test and performing well. Speaking between adults also endowed him with authority. Felipe noted that he felt he knew more Spanish, credited to his ability to translate difficult phrases or semantics from English to Spanish and from Spanish to English. It certainly was a test of his bilingual repertoire in translating in the moment, but also of making sense between adults, and, as he said, "doing a good thing" by helping both people. It is telling that Felipe described the memory of his language brokering as "doing something good" to open the lines of communication.

When I asked Felipe if he had ever watched Guadalupe conduct herself in English in public without his help, he said "sometimes people can't hear her when she talks." Felipe credited this to his mother's "soft voice" in English. Guadalupe's voice in Spanish, though, he said, was "not soft." Felipe further clarified his statement about her English by saying that Guadalupe spoke "loud enough," but people couldn't hear her because of her accent, or that "they can't hear her like the way I do." Several MANOS students expressed similar feelings about these situations in the contact zones of asymmetrical power relations they encountered with their parents in public domains. Nevertheless, the sense of power, of "doing something good" to help his mother, empowered Felipe to think positive of his ability to language broker for the family, and as part of his family duty when called upon. For students like Felipe, activities to help build on this sense of positive association would increase comprehension of audience with bilingual activity.

When the MANOS language brokers assisted their parents in coping with English, the family "role reversal" was not a dramatic turn: children helped their parents and considered it as nothing more than helping out around the home or—

if outside the home—as helping with home matters that contribute to the overall well-being of home life in the family. The example of Felipe's memory of language brokering for his mother illustrated this. Felipe's language brokering for his mother permitted him not only to extend his emerging biliteracy and bilingualism to her, but also to understand the practicality of language uses in his family and his special place as facilitator. He gained responsibility in his family because he used his bilingualism as a service to his household. Orellana's extensive longitudinal research with language brokers speaks to similar strengths immigrant youth acquire as they overcome moving between languages and helping their families. In the next section, I offer a language brokering narrative of a son helping his mother in detail.

Language Brokers Negotiating Literacies and Languages

In this section, I offer a vignette from my fieldwork at MANOS demonstrating language brokering in the everyday practices of a mother and son communicating together for specific ends. The setting was a Cinco de Mayo celebration sponsored by a Latino student group at a local university and held outside the university library's quad. Several of the members of the student group were also MANOS tutors. Together with MANOS, the students organized an event to celebrate Mexican culture on campus. The MANOS families helped to organize the entertainment and food vendors. The results on the steps before the campus library were Mexican folklórico and Aztec performance dancers, mariachis, poetry, and plenty of food vendors—including a taco truck from the neighborhood. I was reminded of some of the Cinco de Mayo celebrations I used to attend growing up in Arizona—though nothing quite like this one experienced on a college campus in New York City.

Several MANOS mothers pooled money together to prepare large batches of tamales and tostadas to sell at the event. One mother, 31-year-old Juana, set up a beauty care products table. Her son, eleven-year-old Luis, helped her with the suitcase, and also with setting up the intricacies of the display, as if he had done so before. I approached them and asked them how they were.

Juana, always cheerful, said hello to me, and we shook hands. I shook hands with Luis next and said hello. I said it was nice to see him giving his mother a hand.

"Sí verdad, Luis es un buen ayudante a su mama" (Yes it's true, Luis is a good assistant to his mother).

"She said I help her."

Juana was pretty much always able to understand my English. I could say things to her in English, and she would usually respond in Spanish, but sometimes in English. She often would use MANOS tutoring sessions with her sons to practice her English. She also spoke a good deal of English in her work as a housecleaner in Manhattan. Juana had attended school up to the eighth grade in Puebla, Mexico, but as the oldest child, she claimed it was her duty to forgo further education to help financially support her younger siblings. First, she migrated to Mexico City working domestic jobs there, but eventually found her way to New York City. Through her financial support to her family, all of her younger siblings have completed high school, and one graduated with a degree in education from college. When her boys

Luis, and four-year-old Pablo were older, she hoped to complete her education, and eventually earn her college degree, before returning back to Mexico. Juana had begun selling cosmetics within the last six months as a way to earn some extra money working from home on weekends and some evenings. Her best customers were the mothers of MANOS, as well as the mothers at another after-school program just up the block from the program.

Juana and Luis both fielded and answered questions from interested browsers of her wares. I sat near them and observed Luis handle all the English language brokering duties for Juana, and how together they counted money and made change. One customer asked about the ingredients of some lotions, turning her attention between Juana and Luis. Juana held the bottle and read some of the ingredients, but then checked them with Luis, who read them, and then with the customer who read them. The customer made some comment about aloe content, which neither Juana nor Luis were sure about, but Luis pointed out that a different version of the lotion was very popular. He began in Spanish then corrected himself: "Claro—esta—señora—es muy rica: you must smell this—"

Luis then told the customer that there was no aloe in this type of lotion, but that his mother highly recommended it for its smell.

Juana said to Luis, "dile que lo pruebe" (tell her to try it). Juana gestured applying the lotion with her hands.

"You can try it, too. It smells very good," Luis said to the customer.

"Me gusta mucho este," said Juana.

"My mom says she likes this one a lot."

"Such a good sales team," the customer said with a smile, and she purchased the bottle of lotion.

The two made a solid team. After I asked Luis how he liked helping his mom with work. "It's fun because I can try to sell stuff and help my mom because sometimes she can't talk to the people who speak English, and I can talk to them to help her." For his effort, Juana gave a portion of each sale to her son.

Luis not only helped his mother with the transaction, but he also predicted how to approach his audience with practices he learned along with his mother. The move to smell the popular lotion was one Juana taught Luis, both explicitly and through practice with audiences she sold to in Spanish. During this day at the college, however, the sales team came into contact with a significant amount of English-speaking customers. For this reason, Luis's ability to negotiate languages and sales pitches became extremely important. Together, Juana and Luis did well to collaborate bilingually for the well-being of the family, but also for the caring togetherness of parent and child supporting one another.

From Theory to Practice: Schooling Values and Valuing Families

The setting for language brokering at MANOS involved bilingual youths mediating institutional and family literacy in a constellation of homework texts in Spanish and English, which in turn produced constellations of effects in their daily lives. The acts of language brokering in the case of the bilingual youths at MANOS were bilingual contacts between institutional and familial languages. In facilitating this communication, the youths who gained the potential to feel empowered as language brokers in their families. Without assurance and mentorship, language broker youth might turn to the dominant language and internalize a perceived "lack" in the home literacies, imposing a type of self-censorship and relying less and less on the home language as a form of everyday communication. Over the course of another generation or two, this eventually results in home language loss among immigrant families. Future research into language brokering should probe deeper into how transitions between language dominance in immigrant families. Research in such cases must examine linguistic power dynamics over extended periods of time and into actions that reduce language loss over the second and third generations.

MANOS's community literacy program, for some parents in the neighborhood, served as a last and only resort to do something for their children. It also functioned as a protected site away from the schools, where parents aired their grievances with their children's' schools, where parents could learn about schools without having to interact with school officials who intimidated and embarrassed them for not speaking English. The ease of speaking in Spanish, of course, facilitated this most. In *Language and Symbolic Power*, Pierre Bourdieu examines linguistic exchange as an always already structured interaction whose form and content carry certain ascribed levels of value or distinction. According to this framework, differently valued forms of speech and writing structure the internalized forms of self-imposed censorship experienced at the human level. In the case of language brokering, youths redistribute the values of languages more equitably. There is power in this, and certainly when considering the power of immigrant families to communicate collectively.

For language-minoritized families, the standardized academic English literacy required by schooling necessarily entails language brokering and power inequalities. This ability to redistribute linguistic inequalities permits non-English individuals to broker linguistic capital in the linguistic marketplace, and I argue language brokers profit in a number of ways. Their possession of English in their families signifies Bourdieu's notion of *ethos* as "a sign of status intended to be evaluated and appreciated," a "sign of authority, intended to be believed and obeyed" (66). At other times, this caused pressure and sometimes emotional pain when children felt ashamed for their parents' nonstandard English accents. Sometimes this accounted for a rapid transition to English dominance in the second generation and eventual heritage language loss.

Teaching Strategies to Reach Language Brokers
Understanding the practices of bilingual students in their families is a necessary undertaking for all educators. Barely recognized or integrated into school-based language arts, the language brokering performed by youth language brokers has a community-based language function rewarded and cultivated only outside school. Lisa M. Dorner et al. find in their sample that "higher levels of language brokering were significantly linked to better scores on fifth- and sixth-grade standardized reading tests" (451). These translingual types of classroom practices can extend from

bilingual classrooms and into language arts in K-12, and even into university writing classes. Language brokering could be emphasized in schools with bilingual students as an untapped potential for empowering students and improving development of crafting voice in writing. Of course, more research must be performed to determine fully which aspects language brokering improves and how standardized testing scores intersect with specific aspects of the literacy activity. As it stands, however, language brokering and translation happen every day for immigrant families, and not as something learned by students for a test. School tests, however, do constantly remind students learning English about the social relations between their home languages and those preferred by institutions. For example, the MANOS youths learned about the social relations between Spanish and English within New York City, and their accents among the seas of those around them. MANOS youth language brokers also observed how their parents' nonstandard English accents marked them as immigrants in the U.S. mainstream. This proved to be a difficult issue for some to fully comprehend, and they sometimes leveled blame at their parents for their Spanish dominance. MANOS students had acute ears for accents in English and Spanish, and as material for study, language brokers would no doubt demonstrate higher levels of comprehension for registers of voices. In this sense, this very important translanguaging activity deserves further invitation into school curricula. Until then, however, it is important to examine language brokering as it happens in communities of practice. In terms of intersections of life and study, ethnographic projects exploring student communities, languages, accents, and literacies encapsulate methods for students to discover data from their experiences for analysis.

There are a number of immediate and structural ways schools can tap into the potential of language brokers in classrooms and pedagogy. For the sake of immediacy, I offer two pedagogical outlines instructors could employ right away in language arts classrooms. These methods seek to utilize and promote students' bilingualism and biliteracies in their classrooms as sources for study, and to increase student engagement in conducting self-led research community projects that seek to sustain bilingual practices rather than assimilate monolingual assumptions about language standardization.

Educators should acknowledge the academic potential for studying translation and student autobiographies of spoken and written registers. Writing courses at all levels stand to gain by incorporating ethnography and autoethnography projects that take students into communities to conduct field research. Students' interviews should be transcribed with attention to accents and translations when necessary. *On Ethnography: Approaches to Language and Literacy Research* by Shirley Brice Heath and Brian J. Street offers an excellent primer to conducting student research projects studying literacies and learning. To further gain social perspectives, ethnographic projects should involve groups of students from different backgrounds each taking part in researching the homes and languages of classmates for writing. In such shared projects, students conduct fieldwork and write about the lived experiences of communities. They practice critical thinking skills applied to researching their lives and their rich, experiences. The results are relevant writing projects rooted in students' real lives.

Student-teachers in this model would develop their own educational skills by using ethnographic fieldwork, from which they derive the themes and words of special consequence to the targeted population. Ethnographic methods research can tap into pedagogical value of local language uses and theoretical rigor. For future instructors, ethnography is clearly a valuable learning tool. From a critical point of view, student researchers would come to note how dominant and minority languages interact through the bilingual practices of agents moving between languages, especially at the family level, but also in communities. Speculations into how power dynamics function between children's and adults' access to—and possession of—the dominant literacy would necessarily extend the scope of teacher training to examine how and why families sharing a common situation coalesce to address their interests and needs. This would also offer important insight to future instructors about the strengths students and their families bring to classrooms, complicating a one-dimensional stereotype of low-income immigrants as dependent vessels of deficits needing to be filled with the so-called "official" language.

At the moment, it is important to first understand that language brokering is a phenomena resulting from a variety of historical and social factors, but that it has occurred for thousands of years, as long as cultures have migrated across the globe. Language brokering is an everyday literacy practice, but one that in the United States gets relegated to outside classrooms. Encouraging language brokering inside classrooms is the beginning to recognizing it as a tool for student involvement and multicultural interest. As multilingualism and globalization continue to shape one another, all students will develop multilingual proficiencies. To begin now, however, teachers can begin by inviting language brokering into lessons. For example, teachers requesting translations from different languages into English from other languages during class lectures is a way to empower emergent bilingual students to speak, and with the authority of another language. Language brokering highlights student translation in context with conversations at hand, but it also lends esteem to the academic ability to speak of certain subjects in the classroom in languages not English.

In addition, activities that could require translation assurance, as in bilingual versions of poems, also can be places where instructors can ask students experienced as language brokers to further engage in class. When using media for analysis, finding those with subtitles in different languages can also invite participation from language brokers. Looking at examples of commercials from other parts of the world can become fruitful material for rhetorical analysis in a defamiliarized linguistic context. Students familiar with the language and culture in foreign commercials can become sources of authority for fielding questions from students and teachers. Questions of cultural difference could be researched into topics of comparative political or cultural issues.

Analysts and educators would serve this diverse society well by penetrating "smokescreens" attempting to segregate languages through politics, a project the linguist Ana Celia Zentella described two decades ago as teaching and learning from sociolinguistic inequalities. Zentella argues that the "language smokescreen that obscures ideological, structural, and political impediments to equity" can be used to examine the macro picture of Spanish as a historically thriving language in the United

States (9). The anthro-political perspective—as Zentella terms it—is strongly allied with the precepts of critical or applied anthropology, as well as with critical discourse analysis and a Freirean pedagogy of empowerment from the grassroots. Following the anthro-political motivations for scholarly research set forth by Zentella, one hope for my research is to open teachers and parents to the existence of multiple routes to bilingualism, biliteracy, and language education.

Works Cited

Alvarez, Steven. "Translanguaging Tareas: Emergent Bilingual Youth Language Brokering Homework in Immigrant Families." *Language Arts*, 91. 5 (2014): 326–39.

Bourdieu, Pierre. *Language and Symbolic Power*, edited by John B. Thompson, translated by Gino Raymond and Matthew Adamson. Cambridge: Harvard UP, 1999. Print.

Corsaro, William A. *The Sociology of Childhood*. 2nd ed. Thousand Oaks: SAGE, 2005. Print.

Dorner, Lisa M., et al. "'I Helped My Mom,' and It Helped Me: Translating the Skills of Language Brokers into Improved Standardized Test Scores." *American Journal of Education*, vol. 113, no. 3, 2007, pp. 451-478.

Heath, Shirley Brice. *Ways with Words: Language, Life, and Work in Communities and Classrooms*. New York: Cambridge UP, 1983. Print.

Heath, Shirley Brice, and Brian V. Street. *On Ethnography: Approaches to Language and Literacy Research*. New York: Teachers College P, 2008. Print.

Jones, Curtis J., and Edison J. Trickett. "Immigrant Adolescents Behaving as Culture Brokers: A Study of Families from the Former Soviet Union." *Journal of Social Psychology*, 145. 4 (2005): 405–27. Print.

Latino Data Project. "The Latino Population of New York City, 1990–2010." City U of New York Center for Latin American Caribbean, and Latino Studies, 2011.

Orellana, Marjorie Faulstich. *Translating Childhoods: Immigrant Youth, Language, and Culture*. New Brunswick: Rutgers UP, 2009. Print.

Orellana, Marjorie Faulstich, and Ofelia García. "Language Brokering and Translanguaging in School." *Language Arts*, 91. 5 (2014) 386–92.

Orellana, Marjorie Faulstich, and Jennifer F. Reynolds. "Cultural Modeling: Leveraging Bilingual Skills for School Paraphrasing Tasks." *Reading Research Quarterly*, 43.1 (2008): 48–65. Print.

Orellana, Marjorie Faulstich, et al. "In Other Words: Translating or 'Para-Phrasing' as Family Literacy Practice in Immigrant Households." *Reading Research Quarterly*, 38. 1 (2003): 12–34. Print.

Puig, Maria Elena. "The Adultification of Refugee Children: Implications for Cross-Cultural Social Work Practice." *Journal of Human Behavior in the Social Environment*, 5. 4 (2002): 85–95. Print.

Smith, Robert C. *Mexican New York: Transnational Lives of New Immigrants.* Oakland: U of California P, 2006. Print.

Suárez-Orozco, Carola, and Marcelo M. Suárez-Orozco. *Children of Immigration.* Cambridge: Harvard UP, 2001. Print.

Tse, Lucy. "Language Brokering Among Latino Adolescents: Prevalence, Attitudes, and School Performance." *Hispanic Journal of Behavioral Sciences*, 17. 2 (1995): 180–93. Print.

Valdés, Guadalupe. *Expanding Definitions of Giftedness: The Case of Young Interpreters from Immigrant Communities.* Mahwah, NJ: Lawrence Erlbaum P, 2003. Print.

Weisskirch, Robert S. "Feelings About Language Brokering and Family Relations Among Mexican American Early Adolescents." *Journal of Early Adolescence*, 27. 1 (2007): 545–61. Print.

Zentella, Ana Celia. *Growing Up Bilingual: Puerto Rican Children in New York.* Malden, MA: Blackwell Publishers Ltd., 1997. Print.

Author Bio

Steven Alvarez is Assistant Professor of English and Coordinator of the First-Year Writing Program at St. John's University. He specializes in literacy studies and bilingual education with a focus on Mexican immigrant communities.

"My Little English": a Case Study of Decolonial Perspectives on Discourse in an After-School Program for Refugee Youth

Michael T. MacDonald

Abstract

Literacy "sponsorship" in refugee communities is not without its risks and limitations. For potential sponsors, risks include the commodification of refugee voices, while limits include inaccurate generalizations of those being sponsored. This essay draws from a case study of refugee student discourse to discuss how a more explicit *decolonial* approach to sponsorship can help sponsors rethink a giver-receiver paradigm. This approach would first deconstruct imperialist discourses of power and then replace them with new, alternatives to meaning-making. While contingent on local contexts, this study aims to set an agenda for continued debate within refugee community literacy support projects.

Keywords: refugee, decolonial, sponsorship, discourse, commodification, neoliberalism

> *They had special names for people like refugees from different countries. It's almost like they kind of know you because of your struggles with the language.*
>
> (Michelle, on her experience going to school in a South African refugee camp)

"We Are From Africa! We Do Not Write!"

When I first met the students in this case study, I was a volunteer tutor in an after-school program designed to serve refugee and immigrant youth from the African continent. The majority of students were resettled refugees from Somalia who identified as Somali Bantu. Others were from places like Eritrea, South Sudan, and the Democratic Republic of the Congo. The Somali Bantu students were in high school at the time, but before coming to the U.S., few had limited access to formal schooling. Aid workers reported that when the students were resettled, they were placed into classes according to their age rather than their academic level, which made it difficult for them to catch up on subjects and learn English at the same time. The afterschool program had become an important part of their new relationship with English literacy.

One day, I was working with a student who had a particularly sharp sense of humor, once telling me—despite him being only seventeen—that he had been a background dancer in the video for Michael Jackson's *Thriller*. He would often challenge people to dance contests. While going over some reading response questions, he became frustrated. He pushed his chair back, threw up his hands, and exclaimed, "We are from Africa! We do not write!" We laughed and moved on, but for me, his statement came to embody the intersection of competing discourses educators, politicians, aid workers, and volunteers use to describe the educational histories of refugee students. By parodying back to me statements others have made of students like him, he both identified the colonizing discourse of literacy and talked back to it.

In her reflection on decolonizing research methodologies, Linda Tuhiwai Smith observes how literacy has been a primary medium of imperial rationality. While literacy has often been presented as a catalyst for opportunity, only certain kinds of literacy have been valued (English, written), and it has instead represented for many colonized peoples a double-standard and an artificial measure of development:

> Writing or literacy, in a very traditional sense of the word, has been used to determine the breaks between the past and the present, the beginning of history and the development of theory. Writing has been viewed as the mark of a superior civilization and other societies have been judged, by this view, to be incapable of thinking critically and objectively, or having distance from ideas and emotions. (30)

These are the colonial contexts from which refugees are resettled. They are also the neocolonial beliefs with which sponsorship is realized. That is, sponsors, despite the best of intentions, risk constructing those they sponsor according to colonial discourse, not necessarily out of ignorance (though sometimes that can be the case), but because an imperialist view of literacy as a "mark" of superiority is the dominant discourse in which we work.

The support and promotion of literacy—or what Deborah Brandt (1998) has termed "literacy sponsorship"—provides an important theory for understanding the materiality and circulation of literacy. Within the sponsorship framework, isolated language practice is not so much important as is the relationships by which those practices are made possible. In refugee communities, sponsorship is comprised of a complex network of stakeholders, each having a vested interest in the sponsorship of literacy in refugee communities. While the impulse to sponsor comes from a place of good intentions, the impulse itself is driven by an imperial rationality that uses literacy, English written literacy in particular, as a "mark" of a superior form of progress and development.

In order to make space within the giver-beneficiary sponsorship paradigm, a more explicitly *decolonial* approach is needed, one that first deconstructs imperialist discourses of power and then replaces them with new, alternatives to meaning making (see Smith). This essay provides one case study of refugee student discourse gathered from interviews conducted in an after-school program. However, it should be noted that as a researcher, I have put myself in a questionable position—the fact that I am a white, English-speaking, academic attempting to use a decolonial approach to analyze refugee discourse has me playing a similar role to that I aim to critique. I hope to make my methods and interpretations open to questioning. My positionality represents a microcosm of the central problem this essay addresses: literacy sponsorship in refugee communities, while well-intentioned, is a primary means of circulation for the discourses of power that prevent refugees from actualizing sovereignty and participating fully in self-governance. In short, refugees are cast as a "problem" to be fixed (Lui, 116) rather than as providing important resources and solutions to the inadequate institutions of education. In this case study, refugee students identify and speak back to the neocolonial discourses that govern their encounters with English literacy. Close attention to these discursive moments can point to ways in which sponsors might cultivate a decolonial perspective, one that disrupts discourses of power, shifts the paradigm of sponsorship, and makes space for new and radical knowledges.

Decolonizing Discourse and Paradigms of Sponsorship

While the idea of literacy sponsorship here is the focus of my critique, it must be acknowledged that literacy can also provide a powerful means of awareness and resistance. But, unreflectively entering a marginalized and vulnerable community with a perspective informed by a "rhetoric of liberation" (Smith, 75) is a problem; it is short-sighted at best and oppressive at worst to assume that merely supporting English literacy in refugee communities will "lift" those communities up and out of economic poverty, remove them from the scrutiny of public suspicion, and restore political self-determination. As sponsors—composition teacher-scholars, literacy researchers, and community activists—we must be willing to ask the question as to whether it is even possible for us to shift the sponsorship paradigm away from colonizing discourses. It must also be noted that many sponsors are from indigenous and refugee communities, and working with them would be an important opportunity for future research on community literacy. Institutional structures of sponsorship, however, like university-community partnerships, need more radical perspectives in positions of power, and this is one potentially overgeneralized assumption from which my critique begins.

A decolonial perspective can be thought of as requiring at least two approaches: the identification of colonizing knowledges and the advocacy of new ways of imagining the world that are specifically informed by indigenous experiences. This second point is why sponsors might have difficulty transforming sponsorship on their own. Pan-African studies scholar Sabeb J. Ndlovu-Gatsheni, for instance, calls the decolonial approach an "epistemic perspective," arguing that it expresses "counter-hegemonic intellectual thought" that "opens up the invisible global imperial designs embodied by modernity" (386-87). *Modernity* in this case represents the perceived distance between literacy sponsors and refugee communities, the catching-up students might have to do, and the ways in which sponsors perceive a refugee's educational background. Such "designs" of distance have historically sought to "classify and name the world" in asymmetrical ways (388). Contemporary imperial designs are engaged through neoliberal rationalities, free market obsessions, and as Ndlovu-Gatsheni notes, the "deployment of democracy" rather than advocacy for equality (391).

For Smith, a decolonial perspective identifies the "order"—the underlying "code" and "grammar" of imperialism, a code that has, in fact, generated "disorder" and "fragmentation" in the lives of indigenous peoples (29). Smith critiques Western academic traditions for constructing artificial "binary categories" and regarding history as a "totalizing discourse" that is all-encompassing rather than nuanced, subtle, and contingent (30-31). In composition and rhetoric studies, Ellen Cushman also adopts a decolonial perspective and identifies a need for the examination of "dualistic thinking ... because it maintains the center/periphery of knowledge-making efforts" (239). Imperial constructions of knowledge dictate what discourses are possible in a given context, and scholars like Smith argue that real critique of imperial discourse cannot be conducted without the explicit inclusion of indigenous voices. If western academics are embedded within these totalizing discourses, then indigenous perspectives remain *outside* these established knowledge regimes and as a result, can offer alternative strategies not possible within the imperial paradigm.

Sponsorship is not exempt from imperial discourse and can reinforce asymmetrical relations of power between the sponsor and sponsored. As Brandt notes in her oft-cited definition, sponsorship involves the regulation and suppression of literacy just as much as it supports and enables it (166). A decolonial approach to literacy sponsorship in refugee communities would question literacy as a "criterion for assessing the development of a society" (Smith, 33). It would embrace what Cushman calls "pluriversal realities" of language, literacy, and lived-experience (235). It would defy categorization that is based on linear, developmental models wherein those who are literate sponsor those perceived to be illiterate. From this view, sponsorship appears more akin to a kind of corporate sponsorship, regulated by neoliberal expectations of behavior. If performances of literacy do not meet the neoliberal prerequisites of English, then the sponsored are deemed "ineducable," "troublesome," and "delinquent" (Smith, 67). Instead, as Cushman proposes, "Understanding the differences within difference as the norms of all utterances" can open up new forms of meaning making (238).

Acts of sponsorship also are prone to what Leigh Patel identifies as "compartmentalization," or the understanding of "parts at the expense of the whole" (19). Focusing on English literacy acquisition rather than on a multilingual whole, or on individual literacy practice rather than on systemic educational deficiencies puts an undue burden on the sponsored, positions them as a problem to be solved rather than as part of a holistic solution. Perhaps viewing difference as a norm can shift the sponsorship paradigm so that those who are sponsored, like refugee students who live and learn in vulnerable communities, are not treated as problems, but as leaders and problem-solvers.

Methods and Reflection

The after-school program took place in a mid-sized, Midwestern city that had been a primary resettlement location for several groups of refugees. The organization within which the program was housed had a strong commitment to serving groups from the African continent in particular. And, during my time there, the city saw an influx of refugees from Somalia and Eritrea.

The students I interviewed—Ali, Musa, and Michelle—were in high school at the time of the study. Ali and Musa had just turned 18, each having the same assigned birthday of January first. They had come to the U.S. at a late enough age to remember their resettlement, including what it was like to learn English for the first time. One of the most important findings that came out of working with them was learning how they responded to the assumptions that circulated about them. When I told Ali, for example, that I would be reporting my research specifically to an *academic* audience, he laughed and said, "Tell them you have a real, live African guy."

Michelle was a sophomore at the time who excelled in her English classes, but told me she struggled with math. She eventually became a tutor herself at the program and was very involved in summer mentorship activities. She was born in the Democratic Republic of the Congo, but after being forced to flee, lived much of her life in a South African refugee camp. She often talked about how her mother would use writing as a form of therapy, as a way to make sense of the disjuncture in their lives.

I frame this essay as a case study of discourse in order to "establish a framework for discussion" (Yin 2) and place emphasis on the "exact words used by" my participants (60).

My use of interviews as the source material for this discourse comes with some limitations. Most concerning is the risk of uncritically celebrating, fetishizing, or commodifying refugee student voices. Janet Bye attempts to clarify some of these problematics in her post-structural analysis of education reform, emphasizing an important distinction between the individual voice of the *subject* and discourse. According to Bye, focusing specifically on discourse can "provide important opportunities to observe the individual being constituted as a subject of neoliberal education" (401). Similarly, my aim is to treat student interviews *as texts* in order to identify discourse that appears to reject, challenge, and question, or accept and accommodate the sponsorship paradigm.

Another guiding principle for this case study has been my ongoing understanding of representation, particularly as described by Trinh T. Minh-ha (2004) in her exploration of researcher self-reflexivity. Trinh argues that self-reflection can only be productive when it goes "beyond" the self in order to identify "established forms," norms, and dominant discourse (235). I keep returning to Trinh's ideas in relation to my own positionality as a white, American, monolingual (I'm embarrassed to admit), academic, cis-gendered man, who was also a first-generation college student from a white working-class family in a small town. This positionality is important to account for, but should not overdetermine my analysis of discourse. One way I attempt to remain consistent with Trinh's argument is by treating my findings and generalizations with caution. For example, rather than take a statement like, "We do not write," as evidence of a generalization or a confirmation of written literacy superiority, I have tried to look for the possible parody and appropriation in the discourse and think about what kind of interpretations the discourse is pointing toward. As a case study, this essay does not pretend to come to definitive conclusions about literacy sponsorship in refugee communities. It only attempts to identify problems and responses to those problems that are already present in the interview texts.

"We Have to Speak It"

While most of this study's examples draw from interviews, my daily interactions with students added to my understanding of their senses of humor, their daily frustrations, and the kinds of relationships they were forming—at least during the time they were in the after-school program. Many of the students came to the program everyday the program was open, and their schoolwork included a wide range of activities. One of my favorite moments was reading *Romeo and Juliet* with one student, who, once we both looked up the annotations to the text, quickly grasped the humor and kept shaking his head in disbelief at the characters' actions.

At other times, students appeared to appropriate discourses of power, reflecting in some ways the "literate arts of the contact zone" (Pratt, 37). That is, students seemed to subvert dominant depictions made of them by drawing on practices such as, "autoethnography, transculturation, critique, collaboration, bilingualism," as well as multilingualism and "parody" (37). Statements like, "We do not write" and "Tell them you have a real, live African guy," often took the form of cutting or self-deprecating remarks. On several occasions, the Bantu students asked me—and sometimes the other tutors—if I liked bugs on my pizza, saying that that they would always eat bugs when they were in "Africa." They asked me to write them checks for a thousand dollars, a joke that underscored the discourses of aid in their everyday lives. Through these jokes, their audience was forced to see value in rhetorical strategies meant to push them away.

An important "literate art" that spoke back to representations of refugees—Somali Bantu refugees in particular—as having limited or deficient literacy histories was their use of multilingualism. For example, Ali told me that he knew eight languages. Musa said he knew four, and they both spoke with pride about their home languages, particularly Maay Maay. Closely connected to Bantu history, Maay Maay is sometimes symbolic of the marginalization of the Bantu in Somalia. As an ethnic minority, the Bantu were descendent from the indigenous peoples exploited and displaced by continental slave trade (Van Lehman and Eno).

Ali and Musa continued to use Maay Maay with their Bantu peers in the U.S., wanting to preserve the language as part of their identity. Musa said, "My friends like speaking English, but you know, we don't want to lose this language, so we have to speak it." Ali also explained how Maay Maay was like a secret language for him: "We didn't forget it ... We use it and most people say, 'What are you talking about?'" Maay Maay appeared to play a complex role in the after-school program because it united students who had similar linguistic backgrounds, but tutors sometimes talked about how students who were newer to the program, and to the U.S., seemed to feel left out. I cannot comment on this because I only heard positive things about the use of Maay Maay from students and aid workers. The program itself advertised the linguistic diversity of its aid workers and students, and Maay Maay was one important aspect of this message. From a more holistic point of view, this norm of linguistic diversity in their lives reflects the "pluriversal realities" of their encounters with English literacy sponsorship (Cushman 235). A decolonial approach would work to understand these contexts and look to the experiences of Ali and Musa for solutions to systemic problems.

"My Little English"

While students spoke a variety of languages, the three I interviewed each expressed seeing English as an integral part of their future goals. When I asked Ali and Musa about the importance of English in their lives, they agreed with popular sentiments that English literacy would give them access to important opportunities. For example, Musa said, "All over the world, English is a major language ... and that's important because I'm going to be the first one going to college in my family." Many of my discussions with students focused on the subject of English, their memories of learning the language, and their perspectives on its importance.

Ali told me about his initial, but very minimal, exposure to English as a child in Somalia:

> I remember I started learning English in Africa. ... Mommy always say go to school, learn some English, but all I knew was "How are you?" and "I'm fine." That's what I knew. That was my English right there. ... A-B-C, 1-2-3, and count to ten, that's it. That was my English, my little English. And, that's when we came to America.

While they acknowledged the importance of English, Ali and Musa also did not express any particular need for it during their resettlement process. In the discourse of "little English," Ali presents a knowledge of English that positions it alongside other languages rather than as superior to them. His mother tells him to "learn *some* English." The emphasis on English seems understated. In fact, Ali and Musa also spent time in a refugee camp where they learned Arabic. And, because of their Muslim backgrounds, when they came to the U.S., they were enrolled in a Muslim school where both English and Arabic classes were required. Ali and Musa's interviews seem to present a "pluriversal" view of English. It is portrayed as co-existing with rather than *trumping* or foreclosing other languages. Perhaps, their literate lives could be viewed as "translingual" in nature because, in many ways, they show how their language use is not constrained by borders, but is flexible and adaptive (Cushman, 236).

English, of course, played a more dominant role after Ali and Musa were resettled. For example, the immediate impacts of English literacy sponsorship were felt by Ali when his family received help finding housing. He said, "My house was like a library. They prepared everything for us. Books, all that stuff." The presence of books reflected an important "materiality" (Brandt and Clinton) of sponsorship and appeared to show evidence of sponsorship having had happened—aid workers placing books in the house, volunteers donating them. But, this kind of sponsorship also seemed distanced. The materials of literacy were left for the families, but in reality, many of Musa and Ali's family members, the adults especially, did not speak, read, or write even a "little" English. The books were there, but it was *unclear* what resources or access they were providing.

As Patel observes, a holistic approach to decolonizing methodologies seeks to understand how "dynamic systems … function in material contexts" (17). A small detail, like a book donation, can reveal a larger economy of aid and sponsorship wherein the sponsor actively gives and the sponsored is regarded as a passive recipient. Of course, books can provide important resources, but in my limited experience with book donations, I have seen wild inconsistency in their content. When I first started tutoring, the students were meeting in a classroom that had a shelf of donated books; it was like a magazine display rack set up for easy browsing. This rack contained a range of texts that included golf magazines and ESL versions of "classic" novels like Ayn Rand's *Anthem*. Later, when I suggested that people in my graduate program make some small book donations during the holiday season, one of the books I received was about stories of "great explorers." While these examples are anecdotal, I think they show how something as "innocent" and well-intentioned as a book donation needs care and attention on the part of the sponsor.

This brief example of materiality points to inequalities in the sponsorship paradigm and how the concept of sponsorship itself might not encapsulate the entirety of literacy encounters. The stories Ali and Musa told about their initial experiences with literacy in American schools expressed a complex sentiment. For example, Ali told me about attending school for the first time, explaining how, "The school I went to, they weren't teaching me English. They just put a big book in front of me. The teacher didn't talk to me." In contrast to sponsors filling his house with books—a move that invited his participation in English language learning—formal schooling made him feel unwelcome. This feeling is not necessarily apparent from the perspective of materiality. As Katie Vieira argues, an emphasis on "the economic and material aspects of literacy" can be useful, but at the same time, students like Ali and Musa describe experiences where "literacy *also* seeped into their relational and emotional lives" (426). In addition to material sponsorship—books, English and Arabic classes, etc.—Vieira "proposes a deeper investigation of interpersonal literate meaning-making" (426). As a sponsor of literacy, the teacher in Ali's story neither directly supported nor actively withheld literacy. Ali was, instead, ignored, and this affected his interpersonal relationships with sponsors.

By telling this story, Ali identifies a discourse of silence surrounding refugee education. If teachers are not equipped with the training or resources to support refugee students, then students remain silent and invisible. Ali's discourse captures this moment, and in some ways "reclaims" it by juxtaposing silence with voice. As Smith observes, "Reclaiming a voice in this context has also been about reclaiming, reconnecting and reordering those ways of knowing which were submerged, hidden or driven underground" (72). Examining discourse in these examples provides opportunities for literacy sponsors to reflect on the ways in which they themselves might have "submerged" the experiences of those they have tried to sponsor.

"It's Almost Like They Kind of Know You"

Students' struggles with English literacy were not limited to the U.S. For example, Michelle told me about the asymmetrical power relations that existed in the refugee camp where her family lived before being resettled. Michelle was born to a military family in the Democratic Republic of the Congo where she went to a French-speaking school. Civil conflict forced her, her mother, two sisters, and brother to seek refuge in South Africa. Michelle told me how not knowing English marked her as Other in the refugee camp:

> We didn't fit in because kids and older people—if you didn't speak their language, they are just against you. They had special names for people like refugees from different countries. It's almost like they kind of know you because of your struggles with the language so they call you names and stuff.

Even though Michelle was in the multilingual context of a refugee camp, English was the discourse of currency, so it was hard for her to be accepted by students and teachers.

Despite her negative experience in the camp, Michelle had much more exposure to the English language before her resettlement than many of the other students in the after-school program. If her lack of English had marked her as a refugee in South Africa, years later, her South African English accent would mark her in other ways:

> Well all my teachers are positive. I mean they were amazed that I'm from Africa and they like my accent, I guess, most of them are always like, I like your accent and stuff. And they say we should write about us that nobody knows and I wrote about that I was from Africa and everybody was like "really?" And I was like yeah, I'm from Africa. "Oh we thought you were born in America."

Contrast this with Ali's experience and Michelle's previous exposure to English seems not only to prepare her for school, but also appears to grant her citizenship status in the minds of her U.S. sponsors. Two groups of refugees, one from Somalia, one from

South Africa, are perceived completely differently from each other by sponsors before and after their resettlement.

Ali and Musa did not have access to more than a "little" English. Their negative experiences did not begin until they were resettled. But these experiences were complex. In the following excerpt, Musa explains how English simultaneously played an important role in his feelings of marginalization and his increasing sense of belonging:

> I was in fourth grade and I felt kind of different, you know, meeting new people. I felt different because I didn't know the language. ... At first, when I didn't know English, I didn't want to go to school because people didn't know my language, and I didn't know their language. ... And since then, I started learning it, saying the words and hearing things from other people. Then I liked it. I was the first one out of the house, getting onto the bus.

Both Bantu students expressed an appreciation for education that was previously inhibited by not knowing English. What these perceptions imply is that sponsors risk making inferences about a student's history based on English fluency. While assumptions about educational history might be accurate, these assumptions seem to extend to citizenship, as in Michelle's case, implying that relations of sponsorship are not necessarily equitable.

In these instances, the English language appeared as a regulatory force, but it also seemed to have contradictory effects. Michelle, who had previously gone to a French-speaking school, found herself having to trade one colonizing language for another in South Africa. In contrast, Ali and Musa learned English in primarily English-only settings in the U.S., where not knowing the language made them feel like outsiders. As Prendergast observes, the currency of English can act as a "lubricant" for the mobility of people (127). In these cases, English could keep a student like Musa from going to school, or get him to be the "first one out of the house, getting onto the bus."

These students' statements suggest that the power of English literacy in the everyday lives of refugees is asymmetrical and inconsistently manifested. This power can be silencing, but also contradictory. For instance, Musa told me that he liked to write poems in both Maay Maay *and* English, and all three students expressed an interest in reading English language novels. In composition studies, A. Suresh Canagarajah has warned against sweeping arguments about the global dominance of the English language, observing the complexities of power in postcolonial contexts and how "domination is never wholesale" (25). Students in this case study reflected this perspective. They expressed an awareness of the power dynamics of sponsorship and hinted at their strategic resistance to it. Through parody, multilingualism, and storytelling, students demonstrated how they used their literacy practices to engage with the governing powers of English to craft their own "little" Englishes, illustrating the competing and contradictory effects of literacy sponsorship in the contexts of refugee resettlement.

Conclusion: Toward a Decolonial Approach

> "I sincerely believe that a subjective experience can be understood by others." (Frantz Fanon, *Black Skin, White Masks*, 86)

Identifying the discourses of power that limit the radical potential of literacy sponsorship is a necessary component of a decolonial analysis. And while sponsors should engage in self-reflective practices that bring those discursive constructions to the forefront of critique, the voices of students are also necessary for considering perspectives outside of the sponsorship/imperialist framework. Sponsorship, wherein there is an actor who seeks to help someone perceived to be in need of help, is a deeply engrained habit of Western educators, including tutors, volunteers, and others who directly or indirectly support literacy in refugee communities. Embracing the "pluriversal realities" (Cushman, 235) of literacy sponsorship requires more diligent deconstruction of the sponsorship paradigm itself.

Greater inclusion of student discourse is one argument my essay makes, but this is a common observation among community literacy researchers and advocates, so it is worth noting the differences between inclusion, recognition, and reclamation. As Smith argues, "reclaiming" voice involves a commitment to acts of "reconnecting and reordering" (72). Sponsorship needs a dramatic paradigm shift rather than just additive inclusion. Smith argues that only through the reclamation of indigenous voices can systemic, decolonial change take place. That is, unless indigenous and marginalized peoples are in positions where they can contribute meaningfully to research and knowledge, a colonial agenda remains active. In this regard, my own work here only points toward that fact; it is not necessarily able to follow through on it. But, venues like the *Community Literacy Journal* are already poised to support decolonizing methodologies. For instance, Keyword essays like "Adult Literacy" by William Carney, "Qualitative Research" by Stephanie Vie, and "Reciprocity" by Miller, Wheeler, and White engage in deconstructing and demystifying some of the common tropes in community literacy work. Reciprocity, especially, is a term that embraces a decolonial approach to research because it attempts to decenter authority in researcher-subject relationship. These approaches lay the groundwork for radical shifts in perspective.

The "little Englishes" students have crafted show how English sometimes can, in fact, be a *little* thing to students—powerful and regulatory, yes, but also "little" in the sense that English was only part of a broader landscape of governing forces, all of which, big and small, are subject to commodification as well as contradiction. It followed that students prioritized their English literacy-learning accordingly. Those who find themselves to be the perceived objects of sponsorship have much more to contribute to the reworking sponsorship than they are given credit for—or perhaps it is that such a reworking might seem dangerous to those invested in the status quo? In that case, students and others at the receiving end of sponsorship should be given the lead in any possible sponsorship reform projects. What this would look like would depend greatly on local contexts and would rely on the local expertise of community members. I remember when I asked one student if I could interview him about his memories of learning English for the first time. He grinned, and with more than just a touch of sarcasm in his voice said, "Oh, I know all about that."

Works Cited

Brandt, Deborah. "Sponsors of Literacy." *College Composition and Communication* 49.1 (1998): 165-185. Print.

Brandt, Deborah and Katie Clinton. "Limits of the Local: Expanding Perspectives on Literacy as a Social Practice." *Journal of Literacy Research* 34.3 (2002): 337-56, doi: 10.1207/s15548430jlr3403_4

Bye, Janet. "Foucault and the Use of Critique: Breaching the Self-Evidence of Educational Practices." *International Journal of Qualitative Studies* 28.4 (2015): 394-414, doi: 10.1080/09518398.2014.916003

Canagarajah, A. Suresh. *Resisting Linguistic Imperialism in English Teaching*. Oxford, UK: Oxford UP, 1999. Print.

Carney, William. "Keywords: Adult Literacy." *Community Literacy Journal* 4.2 (2010): 100-04. Web.

Cushman, Ellen. "Translingual and Decolonial Approaches to Meaning Making." *College English* 78.3 (2016): 234-42. Print.

Fanon, Frantz. *Black Skin, White Masks*. New York: Grove Press, 1967. Print.

Lui, Robyn. "The International Government of Refugees." *Global Governmentality: Governing International Spaces*. Eds. Wendy Larner and William Walters, London: Routledge, 2004. 116-35. Print.

Miller, Elisabeth, Anne Wheeler, and Stephanie White. "Keywords: Reciprocity." *Community Literacy Journal* 5.2 (2011): 171-77. Web.

Ndlovu-Gatsheni, Sabeb J. "Decolonial Epistemic Perspective and Pan-African Unity in the 21st Century." *The African Union Ten Years After: Solving African Problems with Pan-Africanism and the African Renaissance*. Eds. Mammo Muchie, Phindil Lukhele-Olorunju, and Oghenerobor B. Akpor. South Africa: Africa Institute of South Africa, 2013. 385-409. Print.

Patel, Leigh. *Decolonizing Educational Research: From Ownership to Answerability*. New York: Routledge, 2015. Print.

Pratt, Mary Louise. "Arts of the Contact Zone." *Profession* (1991): 33-40. Web. http://www.jstor.org/stable/25595469?origin=JSTOR-pdf

Prendergast, Catherine. *Buying into English: Language and Investment in the New Capitalist World*. Pittsburgh: U of Pittsburgh P, 2008. Print.

Smith, Linda Tuhiwai. *Decolonizing Methodologies: Research and Indigenous Peoples*. London: U of Otago P, 1999.

Trinh T. Minh-ha. "The Totalizing Quest of Meaning." *Readings in Feminist Rhetorical Theory*. Eds. Karen A. Foss, Sonja K. Foss, and Cindy Griffin. Thousand Oaks: Sage Publications, 2004. 225-38. Print.

Van Lehman, Dan and Omar Eno. "The Somali Bantu: Their History and Culture." *Culture Profile*. Washington, D.C.: Washington, D.C. Center for Applied Linguistics, Cultural Orientation Resource Center, 2003. 1-33. Web. http://files.eric.ed.gov/fulltext/ED482784.pdf

Vie, Stephanie. "Keywords: Qualitative Research." *Community Literacy Journal* 5.1 (2010):175-80. Web.

Vieira, Kate. "Writing Remittances: Migration-Driven Literacy Learning in a Brazilian Homeland." *Research in the Teaching of English* 50.4 (2016): 422-49. Print.

Author's Note:
Student interviews were part of an IRB-approved study, and all student names are pseudonyms.

Author Bio

Michael T. MacDonald is an Assistant Professor of Composition and Rhetoric at the University of Michigan-Dearborn, where he teaches courses in basic writing, literacy, and global studies. His work has appeared in *College English* and is forthcoming in *The Journal of Language, Identity, and Education*.

Looking Outward: Archival Research as Community Engagement

Whitney Douglas

Abstract

This article examines archival research as a generative community literacy practice. Through the example of a community-based project centered on archival research, I examine the increased possibility the archives hold as a site for rhetorical invention based on collaboration that includes contemporary community members *and* the recovered rhetoric of historical figures. I argue that archival research as community literacy practice creates conditions for a communal form of literacy sponsorship and offer a framework for approaching the archives.

Keywords: archives, collaboration, invention, sponsorship, meaning-making, solidarity

Creating with: Archival Research as Community Literacy Practice

As a graduate student at University of Nebraska-Lincoln, I entered the archives with fellow graduate student Eric Turley, our interest in recovery work piqued by the women's rhetoric we were reading in a seminar. We wanted to recover the rhetoric of Doris Stevens, a prominent national suffragist from Nebraska. What we encountered was not only her national-level story, but the stories of local women who had participated in the statewide suffrage movement. After months collaboratively researching in the archives and having energetic discussions about our findings, we began to question what we were creating with the archival materials and for whom we were creating it. Neither of us were originally from Nebraska and yet we were becoming intimately familiar with a major movement in the state's history. However, envisioning something beyond academic genres—the seminar paper, an article, a conference paper, the dissertation, or a book proposal—was difficult.

While considering the necessity of sharing our archival research both in and beyond academic venues, we were introduced to Judith K. Hart (Judy), director of Angels Theatre Company and a coordinator of a grassroots organization called the DeVoted Women Project (DWP). The organization "aimed to reignite an intellectual dialogue regarding the responsibilities and patriotism of the vote by focusing on the suffrage movement," a vision that seemed especially important considering the continual coverage in the media illuminating low voter turnout for national and local elections[1]. General low voter turnout was an issue, but the members of the DWP were most concerned by how few women were exercising their right to vote and found it critical to remind the public, especially women, that women's enfranchisement had been a contentious political issue and not always a protected right. The DWP planned to commission a playwright to compose a play about the national women's suffrage movement that would help them achieve their goals through promoting civil consciousness.

After meeting with Eric and me and learning about the creative suffrage activism that had taken place on the state level, Judy shifted the play's focus to the Nebraska movement to present a more resonant argument for local audiences about the historical and contemporary importance of suffrage. Although excited by the prospect of our archival research circulating in a new way, Eric and I imagined our involvement with the DWP in a limited way: we would share artifacts we had recovered and seminar and conference papers we had written. Instead we learned that deep collaboration was central to any creative and activist work Judy did, and we worked with her, the playwright, actors, costume and set designers, and other community members throughout the drafting, production, and performances of the play *Nebraska Next!*[2]

In this article, I draw on my experience with the DeVoted Women Project in order to demonstrate how archival research can be a generative community literacy practice. Next, I examine two key insights the project work reveals. The first insight is that archives, as sites of collaborative rhetorical invention, can draw on the knowledge and perspectives of contemporary community members *and* the recovery of the rhetoric of historical figures. A second insight is that archival research as community literacy practice is sustained by a form of literacy sponsorship that integrates the knowledge and expertise of both contemporary and historical community members. Drawing on these insights, I end with a framework for engaging in archival research as community literacy practice.

DeVoted Women Project: Serendipity and the Archives

In *Beyond the Archives: Research as a Lived Process*, scholars explore archival research as a knowledge-making activity, yoking the personal and the scholarly as they document the complexities and serendipities of their research experiences and their planned and unplanned methodologies. Encountering the DeVoted Women Project was a serendipitous moment for Eric and me; we met Judy right as we were questioning what was possible for the archival material we had recovered. Our collaboration with the DWP would productively complicate our thinking about what archival research could and perhaps should be. In order to analyze the potential of archival research as community literacy practice, I will first map out our unplanned methodology that resulted from moving our research into the community.

Working with the DWP called on us to re-envision the recovered artifacts through the lens of rhetorical and literacy theories. It also compelled us to continue researching for additional material to more fully immerse ourselves in the suffrage era. For *Nebraska Next!*, we re-read artifacts alongside DWP collaborators to identify themes that reoccurred throughout the historical documents or which resonated with current discussions of political issues. We collectively decided on themes for the play that both illustrated struggles of the suffragists and reflected the present political climate in Nebraska and the nation at large, such as the rural/urban divide; civic literacy and access to information; sustaining political conversations and organizations; social class and civic participation; religion and politics; immigration; the personal and the public; and the role of technology in politics. These themes became the foundation around which the play was written, and helped to recreate and make suffragists' rhetoric accessible and relevant to a contemporary audience.

We envisioned a traveling production wherein we would enter each host community, perform the play, and engage the community in civic dialogue after the performance. Everything—including the director and actors—needed to fit in a minivan for travel across the vast state of Nebraska. The travel aspect led us to take a Brechtian approach, focusing on issues and situations with a production centered on archetypes rather than specific characters. Four actors—three women and a man—played multiple roles throughout the play. The set was minimal and relied on props and a few easels with enlarged artifacts and photographs from the 1914 suffrage campaign. The sixty-five minute play referenced the national suffrage movement and world events during the early twentieth century, but primarily focused on the activist efforts of Nebraska women and men as they worked for state suffrage.

We purposefully integrated archival artifacts into the play so audience members, in a small way, could intimately engage with the material as we had. *Nebraska Next!* included four songs wherein the audience joined the actors singing songs written to popular melodies like "Battle Cry of Freedom," "America the Beautiful," and "Yankee Doodle Dandy." The songs served as transitions between scenes and simultaneously reinforced themes of the play. One scene in the play invited four audience members on stage to read short speeches. The four speeches (two pro-suffrage, two anti-suffrage) were excerpted from recovered speeches and political pamphlets. Having community members recite the speeches in lieu of actors created a break in the play where the audience was directly confronted with the rhetoric circumscribing the issue of suffrage.

At two different points in the play, the actors "campaigned" and distributed suffrage literature to the audience. Each audience member received copies of two political fliers—one that had been distributed by anti-suffragists and the other by suffragists. The fliers "Ten Reasons Why Women Shouldn't Vote" and "Votes for Nebraska Women!" were passed out at political rallies, street meetings, and other public gatherings. The distribution of these fliers, copies of original archival material, provided audience members with tangible artifacts illustrating the rhetoric that had circulated in their communities almost a century earlier and highlighted the dissonance between suffragists and anti-suffragists.

Following the performance, a "second act" invited the audience to stay and talk about the archival material, the current political climate, and civic participation within their community. Conversations differed in every town. In some, audience members shared stories about their mothers, aunts, and grandmothers who were suffragists. Other conversations focused on the lack of women in local politics; the emptiness of contemporary political rhetoric and media coverage; abortion and women's rights to choose; economic inequalities present in the work place; questions about the historical period and the suffragists themselves; and issues for which community members wanted to advocate. After learning about Nebraska suffragists' strategies, some audience members considered the possibility of drawing on the suffragists' strategies to address and advocate for contemporary political issues.

At some performances, local community members were available to facilitate the second act and share their knowledge about suffrage and civic participation in Nebraska. In towns where resources were scarce or unavailable, Judy, Eric, or I facilitated the second act. Audience members frequently expressed surprise at discovering a vibrant suffrage movement had taken place in their state. Audience members frequently asked questions about the origins of the archival material and expressed interest in knowing more about the suffrage movement and specific events and tensions surrounding it. Through *Nebraska Next!*, we were able to convey our enthusiasm for the artifacts we had recovered and direct people to the archives where they could explore the materials firsthand and ideally use the artifacts for new purposes and audiences.

Rhetorical Invention and the Archives

The turn from viewing archives as passive repositories for gathering existing knowledge to conceptualizing archives as active experiments in meaning-making and sites for knowledge creation illuminates how they are inherently dynamic (Kirsch and Rohan VII). This dynamic nature of archives foregrounds the rhetorical nature of history, compelling us to reflect on the complexities of our subjective positions as rhetoricians and the emotions that shape our research as a lived process attending to the intersection of the personal, cultural, and scholarly aspects of our lives (Kirsch and Rohan 3). A nuanced, layered research process that attends to those intersections demands that we might also think about wider audiences and purposes for our findings. If our archival research is conducted with an eye toward academic audiences only, we limit the potential for new knowledge to circulate and hinder the creation of yet newer knowledge. When approaching archival research as a collaborative act of rhetorical invention, we can create new knowledge and representations of that knowledge *alongside* community members.

Excited by our first foray into the archives and the generative discussions held during the reading through boxes of artifacts, Eric and I had agreed to always conduct our archival research in collaboration. In our roles as DeVoted Women Project collaborators, Eric and I re-entered the archives with new questions and a deeper sense of what collaborative research could be. Like the scholars in *Beyond the Archives: Research as a Lived Process*, we had been initially inspired by personal attachments which cultivated the curiosity and intrigue essential for us to do committed, excellent historical research (Kirsch and Rohan 8). However, our experience with the DWP expanded our notion of attachment as we saw richer possibilities when re-visioning our existing research, conducting additional research with *Nebraska Next!* as our focus, and interweaving our personal attachments with those of Nebraskan communities, leading to engagement in collaborative new acts of rhetorical invention.

More importantly, our community attachment pushed us to think of the women whose rhetoric we had recovered as collaborators. Jacqueline Jones Royster and Gesa E. Kirsch advocate that the goals for recovering women's rhetoric should be to identify them as rhetors, showcase their rhetorical contributions, and find "innovative ways to engage with these women both critically and imaginatively in order to enable a more dialogic relationship between past and present, their worlds and ours, their priorities and ours" (14). The suffragists provided us with a blueprint of how to engage Nebraskan citizens across the state, making them contributors to the project not just through their rhetoric but through their lived experiences and knowledge.

Our choice to create a traveling production was inspired by a key activist strategy the suffragists used. The novelty of automobiles at the turn of the century became a useful tool for suffragists to draw wider attention to their cause. Auto tours enabled them to leave Lincoln and Omaha and deliver their political message to communities in surrounding areas and to recruit more suffragists. Two to five decorated automobiles would travel from town to town—typically three or four per day—and deliver a short program, including speeches and songs at each location. Audience participation through singing and speaking was encouraged during presentation of *Nebraska Next!* in order to re-enact how the suffragists engaged the communities they visited as singing was an important strategy used by the suffragists to encourage participation among audiences at auto tours, rallies, and parades.

Before moving to the next town, the suffragists would engage in a dialogue about suffrage with the townspeople—part of the auto tour was reserved for local townspeople to present short prepared remarks in favor of suffrage. Like the community conversations at the end of the auto tours, the second act of *Nebraska Next!* served as impetus for dialogue with audiences across the state about the responsibility of the vote. To determine potential host communities for the play, the DWP used a campaign district map created by the suffragists. As part of their outreach, the Nebraska Women's Suffrage Association (NWSA) divided the state into 15 districts according to travel routes provided by railroads and rivers. We chose one city in each suffrage campaign district in which to perform the play.

By drawing on suffragist strategies of singing, reciting and hearing speeches, collecting and reading political literature, and dialoguing about voting today, *Nebraska Next!* circulated the spirit of women's activism and rhetoric promoted by the NWSA to communities across Nebraska. The play provided a dynamic rendering of rhetorical artifacts that could be presented to a public audience inclusively through audience participation in the theatrical performance, allowing them to draw their own conclusions about the suffrage movement, make their own connections with the current political situation, and participate in archival research as community literacy practice in a small way.

However, the ability of host communities and their members to participate more fully merits further consideration. The DWP letter encouraged community contacts to invite schools and community groups to participate. It was often a single group who brought the production in, thus targeting their students or members. The idea of a play acting as a springboard for civic dialogue that would reach beyond the play into the community was a bit idealistic. In retrospect, the project often lacked solid community liaisons to connect the play to community groups and local concerns. Without this coordination, the play ended up being more of an event rather than part of ongoing community conversations. We recognized the importance of increased networking and inviting community contacts to become collaborators, or, at the very least, a more integral part of the invention process.

While we were able to engage a wider public audience, the audience we reached was comprised of active civic participants; most of the people who attended the performances were already committed voters more interested in learning about the history of state suffrage. The DWP was especially interested in targeting a younger demographic who, according to statistics, were not voting. Some of the performance sites were community colleges and universities hoping to draw students to the performance. The review in the *Lincoln Journal Star* indicated how the play was "preaching to the converted." This fact pushed us to think about how a younger audience accustomed to movies, internet, podcasts, and other new media forms of communication might have been better reached through another medium. We recognize now the importance of including members of the target audience demographic as collaborators, which would magnify the archive's inventive possibilities.

Another issue we encountered was connecting with community members in ways that would sustain ongoing conversations about civic participation, both within the community and ideally across the state. The suffragists worked to create a statewide civic dialogue and political network in the largely rural state of Nebraska and were successful in doing so. Along those lines, Inspired by their success, we too were interested in the possibility of a more networked form of civic dialogue. Originally, we hoped that the play could serve as a piece of a larger community occasion rather than an isolated event. With limited resources and a fairly small group of collaborators, there was much work necessary to revise and finalize the script, make costumes and props, establish venues, and coordinate logistics finalized prior to the performance.

Our engagement with Nebraska community members and the suffragists as collaborators provides a model for thinking about how to engage with future research subjects. If we are working to "forward an enlarged view of rhetoric as a human enterprise" (Royster and Kirsch 98), we ought to enter the archives thinking of them as an expansive site for invention that considers multiple potential collaborators in the experiment of meaning-making and creating knowledge; this includes as collaborators those whose voices and lived experiences are now housed in collections we recover.

(Re)Creating with: Sponsoring Communal Literacy

The creation and staging of *Nebraska Next!* demonstrates the potential archival research, as a community literacy practice, holds for a shift away from the hierarchical form of literacy sponsorship critiqued by Deborah Brandt. In Brandt's examination of literacy as capital, sponsorship is hierarchical, with sponsors being "any agents . . . . who enable, support, teach, and model, as well as recruit, regulate, suppress, or withhold literacy—and gain advantage by it in some way" (556). The sponsor lends their credibility and resources to the sponsored with the likelihood that they stand to benefit from the success of the sponsored (556). However, the sponsor loses the opportunity to gain valuable knowledge and engagement in deeper meaning-making processes, because they are sponsoring from a unidirectional stance, and contributions of the sponsored go unrecognized unless they directly benefit the sponsor.

Situating ourselves as equal collaborators on community-based projects creates the conditions for reciprocal relationships, minimizing the potential for hierarchies to form. Assuming multiple positions in relation to the central idea of the project creates a shared space for open dialogue between participants, for listening to the expertise of various collaborators, and for making possible the opportunity to negotiate ideas and commitments. The idea at the center of the project becomes the sponsor; collaborators assume flexible identities to move in relation to the center. The solidarity that emerges when a shared idea is at the core of a project encourages participants to bring their knowledge and contributions to the circle, working to erode power structures by resisting ranking and instead, aiming to forge interdependency (Cushman 20).

All DWP participants had identities we brought to the project—company director, scholar, public historian, non-profit worker, actor—but we needed to extend ourselves beyond the initial identities and commitments which drew us to the project. When we started meeting with Judy, Eric and I only saw ourselves as graduate students involved in archival research. At times over the duration of the project, we were hesitant when asked to step out of our roles as researchers to draw on experiences as theater-goers, script-readers/respondents, and women's advocates in our local community. The process of collaborative creation made it clear that flexible identities were ultimately one of the factors that brought the project to fruition, as they allowed us to pause, regroup, and loosen or even let go of some individual commitments in order to consider the whole and to create knowledge in more productive ways. Eric and I came to understand that looking out from the archives into the community also entailed a looking out to see beyond traditional notions of our work as scholars.

Each DWP collaborator had specific commitments, but made those visible and worked to acknowledge and account for the commitments of other collaborators. During the drafting of the script, Judy Hart, director of the Angels Theatre Company who forged the collaboration with the DWP, asked each of us which stories, artifacts, or ideas were most important to us. In a conference call conducted with playwright Carson Becker before she wrote a second draft, collaborators asked what her vision was for the movement of the play as well as which artifacts and stories stood out most to her. Early in the process of imagining the narrative arc of the play, some collaborators wanted to include a scene that illustrated tension between a husband and wife over her suffrage activities. The character, as she was envisioned, would be a victim of domestic violence, adding a layer that petitioned for why women needed the vote as well as drawing attention to a contemporary issue. However, Eric and I had not uncovered anything in our archival research which showed or even hinted at such an example. We were committed to giving voice to the movement that had been sitting dormant in the archives for many years. Invested in representing the stories that emerged from the artifacts, Eric and I expressed our concern that the DWP production cast tell the story of the suffrage movement solely by drawing on what could be seen and interpreted in the artifacts.

Several scenes in the play focused on issues Eric and I didn't feel were as central to the suffrage movement as we had conceptualized it; one scene in particular felt too long and in some ways, not as crucial to the story as other shorter scenes. Yet actors and other company members saw the scene as an important moment that would stir audience emotions, and expressed excitement about it. Accustomed to writing in less overtly emotional ways, Eric and I struggled with the rendering of the scene, yet moved to consider why it might be important theatrically and reflected on how our assumptions were coming from our position as graduate students steeped in academic reading and writing. As the aforementioned examples illustrate, DWP collaborators moved back and forth in a give and take relationship with each other as well as shifted in relation to the project. Expertise was ultimately less of a focus, with collaborative contributions and commitment to the central idea being privileged.

Central to archival research as community literacy practice are Freirean notions of solidarity, which scholars like Ellen Cushman have taken up in working with community members outside the university. The work Eric and I did as collaborators on the DeVoted Women Project made possible new representations of knowledge and modes of engagement that wouldn't have emerged without the people we worked with. In the case of the DWP, solidarity existed around the idea summarized in the project's mission statement of "reignit[ing] an intellectual dialogue regarding the responsibilities and patriotism of the vote by focusing on the suffrage movement in Nebraska" ("DeVoted Women Project"). Within this mission statement, the archival research Eric and I contributed was not the sole focus, but it served to help address a local concern raised by an alliance formed of women's advocacy groups in the Lincoln community. The people involved in the planning thus generated the idea that served as the centerpiece around which the solidarity circle was formed. Had Eric and I entered the project with our own research solidly conceptualized and packaged and an unwillingness to think beyond academic genres and audiences, experimental meaning-making and knowledge creation would have been stifled, as would the potential for building relationships with community members—including the suffragists whose rhetoric we had recovered. The recovered portion of Nebraskan women's history and its rhetoric was able to expand in relation to the growing solidarity circle started by The Angels Theatre Company.

Archival research as community literacy practice enables sponsorship to become a multi-directional creative process that builds solidarity through reciprocal relationships around a central idea. In contrast to the hierarchical definition of sponsorship Brandt critiques, the DeVoted Women Project cultivated a shared sense of sponsorship that entailed a back and forth movement of knowledge sharing. In this scheme, collaborators on the DWP served as both sponsors and sponsored at various points in the project's process. While Brandt points to the success a sponsor receives through sponsoring literacy development, the goals of the DWP were not measured by capitalistic terms of success, but in our ability to reach and share with citizens across the state—to engage with the community.

Although the DWP's success was about engaging with communities, we were concerned about the issue of sustaining the project and its aim to foster civic dialogue and advocate for citizens to vote. Judy had other shows to produce and direct, the actors had other theatrical commitments, other collaborators had pressing professional commitments, and Eric and I had graduate school requirements to fulfill. The project and its challenges served as a critical impetus for me to rethink my identity as a scholar and what I want my scholarship to mean and accomplish. I would love to know on future projects in which I collaborate that the sustainability of a project is defined and viable, no matter how long the course of the project might be.

Although sustaining or even expanding the project was not possible, the DeVoted Women Project reflects the profound potential of archival research as community literacy practice. Archives exist within a community and document its histories, and as such call on scholars to cultivate habits of mind that enable us to locate ourselves within our communities. The field of composition and rhetoric has created momentum in recovering the voices and illuminating the rhetorical contributions of women excluded from the rhetorical canon; however, there is a double silence we must confront. By only moving archival work into academic forums, we risk silencing the voices of the past in our communities and from community members with whom we can collaborate and create *alongside*.

Archival research as community literacy practice urges us to look out from the archives with rhetorical awareness of our communities. Creating *alongside* others demands an openness that requires us to look out from the archives to consider what ideas, questions and concerns exist in the local community in relation to archival materials and making those considerations in conversation with community members. It asks us to consider the potential archives hold for recovery work that is conscious of its creative possibilities: the creation of possible representations of recovered artifacts and the creation of reciprocal relationships in solidarity circles.

A Framework for Approaching the Archives

The conditions for creative possibilities can be created through what Jacqueline Jones Royster and Gesa E. Kirsh call *strategic contemplation*, which involves taking into account as much as possible but not evaluating our research or reaching closure too soon (85). Strategic contemplation invites wonder, creativity, and inspiration into the research process and functions recursively (85)—characteristics that can make archival research as community literacy practice as generative as possible. Approaching archival research through a stance of strategic contemplation, we can begin the process by exploring the following questions:

- What connections exist between these artifacts and current community conversations and/or concerns?

- Who in the community is having these conversations and/or addressing or working to resolve these concerns?

- Who else might have a vested interest in these conversations and/or concerns?

- What multiple forms might these artifacts assume and who might want to engage in acts of rhetorical invention to consider possibilities for making the artifacts public and visible?

- How might the community benefit from the artifacts, and in what ways?

By considering these questions, the archival researcher can begin by inviting community members into early conversation about the recovered artifacts and their creative potential, engaging in collaborative invention to determine a central idea around which a solidarity circle might form.

Archival researchers can also prepare to establish reciprocal relationships with collaborators in a solidarity circle by considering the following early in their research:

- Do collaborators foresee power imbalances in the relationships they seek to build as they begin the processes of creating alongside others?

- Where do individual commitments lie in relationship to the vision and carrying out of the project?

- What identities do collaborators bring to the project, and is there a willingness to work beyond expertise and assume multiple positions in relation to the project?

As the project unfolds, collaborators can begin to consider how to draw on the expertise and knowledge from the voices and experiences of those whose rhetoric is being recovered.

Archival research as community literacy practice asks us to reflect on the intersection of the archives, the community, and our professional identities. Rather than viewing university-community relationships as moments when academics can deliver an already theorized or historically contextualized interpretation of archival research to the public or work on a limited basis with community members from our positions of disciplinary expertise, we can instead build relationships and create new knowledge in collaboration. Archival research as community literacy practice provides shared learning and teaching experience for *all* collaborators, laying a foundation for generating additional insights, new public texts, and even new forms of community literacy.

Endnotes

1   The 2004 presidential primary election showed only 21% of registered Nebraska voters went to the polls though that number jumped to 68% for the general election. But a quick look at the 2005 Lincoln city primary election shows that 19.55% of registered voters went to the polls, representing 11.96% of the entire city's population. The general city election was slightly better with a 29.3% turnout rate or 18.3% of the total population of Lincoln, but these numbers do not tell us how many women participated in the election. Because Nebraska does not ask for gender identity upon registration to vote, tracking voting by gender becomes difficult. The Lincoln Lancaster Women's Commission estimated that close to 66% of eligible (over eighteen and registered) women of Lincoln voted in the 2004 general election but only 16.4% of the total eligible women voted in the 2005 city election (Lancaster County Election Commissioner).

2   Our work with The DeVoted Women Project involved more than collaborating to create *Nebraska Next!*, though that is the focus of this piece. In order to raise money to pay the playwright the Angel's Theater Company performed Wendy Lil's *Fighting Days*. An equality day celebration was held at the Lincoln YWCA where Eric and I gave a formal presentation on local suffrage activity.

Works Cited

Brandt, Deborah. "Sponsors of Literacy." *Literacy: A Critical Sourcebook*, edited by Ellen Cushman, Eugene R. Kintgen, Barry M. Kroll, and Mike Rose. Bedford/St. Martin's, 2001, pp. 555–571.

Cushman, Ellen. "The Rhetorician as an Agent of Social Change." *College Composition and Communication*, vol. 47, no. 1, 1996, pp. 7–28.

"DeVoted Women Project" *Angels Theatre Company*, Sept. 2007, www.angelscompany.org/DeVoted/index.htm. Accessed 15 Sept. 2007.

Kirsch, Gesa E., and Liz Rohan, editors. *Beyond the Archives: Research as a Lived Process*. Southern Illinois University Press, 2008.

Kubert, Larry L. "Nebraska Next!' Preaches Voting Message to Converted Audience." *Lincoln Journal Star*, 9 March 2006, p. 3C.

Lancaster County Election Commissioner. Lancaster County, Nebraska, May 2005. www.lincoln.ne.gov/cnty/election/results/resul05a.htm. Accessed 2 Oct. 2005.

Nebraska Next! By Carson Becker, Directed by Judith K Hart, performances by Tammy Meneghini, Lettie Van Hemert, Mary Douglass, Jack Carpenter, Nebraska, March 2006.

Royster, Jacqueline Jones, and Gesa E. Kirsch. *Feminist Rhetorical Practices: New Horizons for Rhetoric, Composition, and Literacy Studies*. Southern Illinois University Press, 2012.

"Ten Reasons Why Women Shouldn't Vote." Flier. Lincoln: Nebraska Woman Suffrage Association. Archives of the Nebraska State Historical Society, Lincoln, NE. 2 Oct. 2005.

"Votes for Nebraska Women." Flier. Lincoln: Nebraska Woman Suffrage Association. Archives of the Nebraska State Historical Society, Lincoln, NE. 2 Oct. 2005.

"Woman Suffrage Campaign Map." Map. Lincoln: Nebraska Woman Suffrage Association. Archives of the Nebraska State Historical Society, Lincoln, NE. 2 Oct. 2005.

Author Bio

Whitney Douglas is an assistant professor of English at Boise State University, teaching classes in feminist and disability rhetorics, literacy studies, and writing theory and pedagogy. Her current research interest centers on creating a pedagogy of equitability.

Who Researches Functional Literacy?

Donita Shaw, Kristen H. Perry, Lyudmyla Ivanyuk, Sarah Tham

Abstract

The purpose of our study was to discover who researches functional literacy. This study was situated within a larger systematic literature review. We searched seven electronic databases and identified 90 sources to answer our larger question regarding how functional literacy is defined and conceptualized as well as the specific question pertinent to this paper. An analytic template guided our data collection. The analysis was completed by using a spreadsheet to examine two levels of institutional affiliation: 1) the larger institution such as a university or government unit, and 2) the department, program, or division within the institution. Findings showed the 209 authors of these 90 sources represent a diverse set of fields. Further, it appears that multidisciplinary research is being conducted. We discuss implications of these findings and call for more interdisciplinary research.

Keywords: functional literacy, interdisciplinary research, adult literacy, workplace literacy, family literacy, health literacy

Many institutions and organizations have a vested interest in literacy. For example, a historical perspective from the 1940s to the 1960s show the Army, Census Bureau, and Office of Education all defined literacy. During World War II, the U.S. Army coined the term functional literacy to indicate adults' ability to use written instructions to adequately perform basic military functions (De Castell et al.). Thereafter, in 1947 and 1952 the Census Bureau identified a certain number of years of schooling as the equivalent of someone who is functionally literate. In 1960 the U.S. Office of Education increased the number of years of schooling to meet the definition. It was during this era that new military, technological, political, and scientific forces and developments propelled a national interest in literacy. Literacy was recognized to be more than an elementary skill; it was important for economic growth and national advancement.

In more recent times the U.S. government has continued to heavily influence our understanding of literacy through the National Literacy Act (NLA, 1991), National Adult Literacy Survey (NALS, 1992), and National Assessment of Adult Literacy (NAAL, 2003). Internationally, the Organization for Economic Co-operation and Development (OECD), along with the United Nations, Educational, Scientific, and Cultural Organization (UNESCO) has provided definitions of what constitutes literacy. A current initiative by OECD, the Program for International Assessment of Adult Competencies (PIAAC), has assessed 10,000 US adults along with adults in 23 countries to better understand the cognitive and workplace skills adults need to perform in our global 21st-century society and economy. Thus our national society in particular and world society at large focus attention on literacy.

Four official definitions (NALS, 1992; NLA, 1991; OECD, 2000; UNESCO, 1978) most commonly are applied to the terms literacy and functional literacy. Because the definitions use both literacy and functional literacy to refer to the same construct, we use both terms in this manuscript. The four definitions have many similarities, and the wording of the NALS/NAAL definition and the National Literacy Act are identical in parts. NALS, the National Literacy Act, and UNESCO all use some form of the word *function* to describe the results of literate activity. Both the National Literacy Act and UNESCO specifically reference both reading and writing of text, as well as mathematical computations. All four definitions situate literacy within the individual and note that literacy is part of individual functioning and development. Interestingly, the two international definitions, OECD/IALS and UNESCO, specifically indicate that literacy is also necessary for functioning in communities and groups, while the two U.S. definitions, NALS and National Literacy Act, only define literacy as an individual ability. Despite definitional similarities, debate about what counts as literacy continues and many scholars have critiqued concepts related to FL (Bernardo; Ntiri). Without an effective definition that is used across contexts, there is a disconnect among researchers, policymakers, and educators.

Not only have institutions and organizations taken a vested interest, people and researchers across the country with specialties in various areas have also contributed to our understanding of literacy. "Workplace literacy" became a priority during the mid-1980s to mid-1990s as employers, labor unions, and policy makers described the essential skills, both individual and team skills, needed for employees to be successful. "Family literacy" is a concept that has changed in connotation. When first used in the 1980s by researchers, family literacy described the sociocultural interplay of literacy engagement between children, parents, and others. Later, family literacy was referred to programmatically; the most nationally known concept of "family literacy" provided basic literacy and parenting instruction for parents and education for the child (Hannon). A newer concept is "health literacy," which focuses on the skills adults need to function in a health system. The term health literacy has meant different things to a variety of people, often causing confusion and debate (Berkman et al.).

Many organizations, fields, policy makers, and researchers have contributed to our understanding of literacy and related literacies, yet much misunderstanding and dispute arise. Functional literacy (hereafter FL) is complex with many players, but we don't know who is researching FL and whether they are working together. Since literacy is a multidimensional phenomenon (Benson; Smith et al.; White), literacy researchers need to be methodical in their investigations and collaborations. The authors of this paper conducted a systematic literature review to better understand essential questions for our field such as "How is functional literacy defined and conceptualized?" Situated within this larger literature review we asked a question pertinent to this particular paper, "Who is researching functional literacy?"

Literature Review

The need for researchers from various disciplines to come together to address complex issues has received growing interest in the scientific community (Aboelela et al.; Lakhani et al.; Townsend et al.). This awareness could be due in part to the fact society has become interested "in holistic perspectives that do not reduce human experience to a single dimension of descriptors" (Aboelela et al. 330). Interdisciplinary thinking is becoming more common and popular than multidisciplinarity (Townsend et al.).

Aboelela et al. completed a systematic literature review on interdisciplinary research and provided the following definition:

> Interdisciplinary research is any study or group of studies undertaken by scholars from two or more distinct scientific disciplines. The research is based on a conceptual model that links or integrates theoretical frameworks from those disciplines, uses study design and methodology that is not limited to any one field, and requires the use of perspectives and skills of the involved disciplines throughout multiple phases of the research process. (341)

As noted in the definition, simply adding a researcher from a different discipline to a research study does not make research interdisciplinary. Interdisciplinary research results when disciplinary borders are crossed through the process of communication and analysis. The borders that are established by a discipline may be assumptions, theories, technology, methods, techniques, or tools. Interdisciplinary research differs from multidisciplinary research, in which "researchers of various disciplines work separately on different aspects of a broad problem" (Lakhani et al. E261). It is further explained that multidisciplinarians may work on solving similar problems in an isolated manner utilizing only that discipline's tools; the borders among and between disciplines are not crossed (Townsend et al.). A three-phase process assists researchers in developing interdisciplinary communities (Siedlock et al.) The first phase allows individuals to explore possibilities and decide if they want further association. Phase two results in accommodating and engaging collaborative practices. The final phase is a deeper, lasting phase of sustained research. Staudinger wrote, "True interdisciplinarity can only arise if all contributing disciplines are respecting each other as equal partners" (335).

Interdisciplinary research is needed in the field of literacy since we draw upon multiple perspectives from various disciplines. For example, psychology and psycholinguistics contribute to a cognitive perspective. Cognitive frameworks "attempt to explain the internal workings of the mind as individuals engage in complex mental activities" (Tracey et al. 109). Due to the complexity of understanding the mind, numerous models and theories work together to explain the varied processes of comprehension and decoding. Anthropology, sociology, and socio-linguistics influence sociocultural and critical perspectives. Sociocultural theories of literacy are "a collection of related theories that include significant emphases on the social and cultural contexts in which literacy is practiced" (Perry 51). Sociocultural perspectives, therefore, reflect beliefs that language (including literacy) "always comes fully attached to 'other stuff': to social relations, cultural models, power and politics, perspectives on experience, values and attitudes, as well as things and places in the world" (Gee *vii*). Critical literacy theories use a political lens to understand literacy and education, specifically the ways ideology and power relationships connect to literacy. In suggesting that literacy involves reading both the *word* and the *world*, Freire conceptualized literacy as the "relationship of learners to the world" (173). Recently, critical perspectives have extended to include issues of agency and identity (e.g., Lewis, Enciso, & Moje). Situated within the field of literacy we have varied disciplines and perspectives, yielding itself well to interdisciplinary research.

In sum we know three theoretical frames drawing upon multiple viewpoints typically guide adult literacy scholarship. Further, we are cognizant the field of adult literacy has numerous players and has been challenged by the lack of a consistent definition of functional literacy, which impacts research, policy, and practice. Research supports the importance and value of interdisciplinary research, yet we know little about interdisciplinary research being conducted in the field of adult literacy. Therefore, through a systematic literature review, we sought to discover who researches functional literacy.

Methodology

We searched seven electronic databases—Google Scholar, ERIC, PsychInfo, Academic Search, Education Full Text, JSTOR, and ProQuest—for the years 2000-2014 using a combination of terms: FL, functional illiteracy, adult basic literacy, adult basic literacy skills, workplace literacy, family literacy, health literacy, assessment, policy, and theory. This initial search resulted in 238 publications. We used several criteria to decide our inclusion of sources. First, we limited our sources to adults, or adolescents who left school, who have low levels of literacy, including English learners. Second, we selected sources that focused on the United States rather than international contexts. Third, we chose to include sources starting in 2000 to allow us to see the transition between two large-scale assessments (NALS and NAAL). Finally, we included peer-reviewed publications, reports from government agencies, and one book; we excluded dissertations, book reviews, and publications not peer-reviewed.

The sources also represented a variety of fields in which researchers have interest in functional literacy, including: (a) literacy/adult literacy/adult basic education, (b) health literacy, (c) workplace literacy, (d) family literacy, (e) assessment, and (f) literacy theory and policy. These categories are not mutually exclusive, however, as one source might represent more than one category, e.g. health literacy and assessment. Our final sample of 90 sources included 82 journal publications, 7 governmental reports, and one book monograph. These sources comprised 41 empirical studies (46%), four reviews (4%), and 31 theoretical or position pieces (34%). The 15 "other" sources (17%) represented (a) overviews of a particular topic, such as workplace literacy, (b) editorial introductions to special journal issues, (c) essays, or (d) governmental (i.e., not peer-reviewed) reports of research. Also included in this category was White's (2011b) book, which compiled several related empirical studies. Table 1 lists the 90 sources and their key topics. To view Table 1, please visit goo.gl/vLv3uy.

The first step of our analysis process was to create a template. Based upon the work of Rogers and Shaenen (2013) and Compton-Lilly, Rogers, and Lewis (2012) we developed an analytical template to use with each source. The template addressed all our research questions in the larger study; in this particular analysis, we target the findings from only one part of the template. To refine the draft template, each co-author completed the template with an individually-selected source, then the group met to discuss areas that needed to be clarified. After two rounds of template development, we finalized decisions about what types of information to include or exclude in certain situations. Thereafter, all four authors read the same four sources per week, with one author assigned to complete the template for a given source. All authors then discussed each source during our weekly research meetings, reviewed its template, and reached consensus about suggested changes. All four authors were actively involved in all phases of research including conceptualization, data collection, and analysis.

We examined two levels of institutional affiliation: (a) the larger institution, such as a university or government unit, and (b) the department, program, or division within the institution. Both levels were important because information at one level sometimes was missing. This information from the template was entered into an Excel spreadsheet, which began the second step of our analysis process. The spreadsheet includes one row per author for each article; thus, an article with one author would have one row, while an article with three authors would have three rows. Next, we included a column for "notes," where we entered information about each article.

One dilemma occurred when an author's affiliation was unlisted, but known to us by professional reputation, inclusion on a different source, or through personal knowledge. Was this author's affiliation therefore truly unknown? After considering (a) using the data as they were provided by each source, (b) adding affiliations where they were known, and (c) doing a broader internet search to fill in the missing data, we chose the first option, as this aligned with other decisions we made regarding information in the templates and spreadsheet.

We created broad categories for affiliations. Education-related fields included "Education/literacy" (literacy programs, curriculum and instruction departments, etc.), "Education/general" (other areas of education, possibly including literacy researchers if this was not clearly identified), and "Psychology" (including Educational Psychology). All healthcare-related fields, including medicine, public health, and pharmacy comprised one category. Authors who were at governmental institutions (e.g., National Center for Education Research, UNESCO) and those who worked for outside organizations, e.g., American Institutes for Research,

ETS, Weststat, were included in the category of "Statistics/research organizations/government." Affiliation categories included:

- Administrative leadership
- Agriculture
- Education/general
- Education/literacy
- Human resources/workforce development
- Librarians
- Marketing/business
- Medicine/health care
- Psychology/ed psych
- Statistics/research organizations/government
- Other
- Unknown

If researchers' affiliations were unknown, they went together into one category. We also identified sources for which there was no author affiliated with literacy or education whatsoever.

It is important to note that an individual author may have multiple sources represented in our analysis. Thus, although there are 209 authors in our analysis, some of these authors are repeated. Similarly, the same author might be represented in different categories, since journals may report affiliations in different ways, or an author who has more than one source may have changed institutions between publications.

We performed this analysis for all of the articles together, and then by our broad topic categories, e.g. health literacy, workplace literacy. For each topic, we reported the counts of different affiliations. Since some articles had combinations of authors in which some affiliations were known and others were not, we also counted the number of articles for that topic for which all of the authors were unknown—this was typically where the journal doesn't note that sort of information. We also counted the number of articles for which there was no author affiliated with literacy or education whatsoever.

Findings: Who Researches FL?

The 209 authors of the 90 sources in our analysis represent a diverse set of fields. Table 2 provides an overview of the institutional affiliations of authors who have written about FL. Medicine and healthcare-related fields have the largest number of authors (47, or 22%). Those working in statistics, independent research organizations, and for the government (39 authors, or 19%) comprised the next largest category. Authors who were generally in education (27, or 13%) and specifically in literacy education (25, or 12%) also represented a large portion of those writing about FL. Other authorial affiliations were less common: eight authors (4%) came from psychology or educational psychology, seven (3%) were from marketing or business departments, four (2%) were in agriculture, and two each were in administrative leadership or academic libraries (1%, respectively). Academics in "other" categories comprised 11 authors; these fields included sociology/survey methods, English, information design, science/technology, Africana studies, writing and rhetoric, and economics.

In addition to counting authors' affiliations, we also accounted for (a) sources in which no affiliations were indicated, and (b) sources in which no literacy or education experts were included among the authors. In many cases, unknown authorial affiliations were due to the fact that journals did not indicate affiliations; however, in some cases, affiliations were indicated for some authors but not others on the same publication. Across all sources, 32 authors' affiliations (15%) were unknown, and 15 sources did not list affiliations for any authors (17%). An astonishing 31 out of 90 sources (34%) listed no literacy or education expert among the authors – and these 31 articles represented only the articles where the authors' affiliations were known! It is, therefore, possible (indeed, even likely) that the percentage of articles with no literacy or education authorship would increase if we included all of the unknown affiliations.

Table 2.
Institutional/Departmental Affiliations of Authors Writing about FL by Topic Area

		All sources	Functional literacy/ABS	Family literacy	Health literacy	Workplace lit.	Assessment	Theory	Policy
Distribution of authors across disciplines/fields	Other	11 (5%)	4 (3%)	0	0	2 (9%)	1 (1%)	0	1 (7%)
	Stats/research/ govt org	39 (19%)	27 (22%)	0	9 (13%)	0	23 (29%)	1 (17%)	2 (14%)
	Psychology/ ed psych	8 (4%)	5 (4%)	0	1 (1%)	0	3 (4%)	0	0
	Medicine/ healthcare	47 (22%)	17 (14%)	0	44 (66%)	0	27 (35%)	0	0
	Marketing/ business	7 (3%)	7 (5%)	0	2 (3%)	0	0	0	0
	Librarians	2 (1%)	0	0	2 (3%)	0	0	0	0
	Human resources/ workforce	2 (1%)	0	0	0	2 (9%)	2 (3%)	0	0
	Education (literacy)	25 (12%)	19 (16%)	2 (25%)	5 (7%)	2 (9%)	6 (8%)	2 (33%)	3 (21%)
	Education (general)	27 (13%)	20 (17%)	6 (50%)	1 (1.5%)	4 (18%)	5 (6%)	3 (50%)	6 (43%)
	Agriculture	4 (2%)	4 (3%)	0	0	0	4 (5%)	0	0
	Admin. leadership	2 (1%)	0	0	0	2 (9%)	0	0	2 (14%)
Overview of authorship	Articles w/ no literacy expert	31 (34%)	14 (12%)	0	15 (75%)	4 (29%)	9 (35%)	0	2 (22%)
	Total # of authors	209	121	12	67	22	78	6	14
	Sources w/ unknown affiliations	15 (17%)	7 (14%)	3 (38%)	1 (5%)	5 (36%)	1 (4%)	0	0
	# of sources	90	51	8	20	14	26	3	9

As Table 2 indicates, we also examined the authorship according to our keyword topics, e.g. health literacy, workplace literacy, assessment, etc.. The 51 sources in our sample that focused upon FL, functional illiteracy, and/or adult basic skills represent 121 authors. The most represented affiliation was statistics, research organizations, and the government, with 27 authors (22%). General education and literacy education affiliations were closely represented, with 20 authors (17%) and 19 authors (16%) respectively. Medical or healthcare fields represented 17 authors (14%). Other fields had fewer than 10 authors each; business and marketing represented seven authors, psychology and educational psychology represented five authors, agriculture represented four authors. Authors in "other" categories included English (2), Africana studies (1), and writing and rhetoric (1). We could not determine the affiliations for 17 authors (14%). Of the 51 sources in this category, 14 (12%) had no literacy or education expert listed among the authors. The trends in findings for the topic of FL and adult basic skills reflect the trends from the overall analysis, with the exception that the proportion of healthcare authors has decreased. These findings suggest that researchers in a wide variety of fields – medicine, business, agriculture, etc. – are interested in adult literacy.

Health Literacy

The 20 sources in this category represented 67 authors. Although medical and healthcare fields dominated the authorship (44 authors, or 66%), the remaining authors were in diverse fields. However, no institutional category had more than 10 authors. Nine authors were in statistical, research, or governmental organizations; five were in literacy education; two each were in business/marketing and academic libraries, and general education and psychology or educational psychology had one each. One important finding for this category is that 15 of the 20 sources (75%) included no literacy or education expert whatsoever.

Workplace Literacy

A total of 14 sources addressed workplace literacy, representing 22 authors: four in general education, and two each in literacy education, human resources and workforce development, and administrative leadership. Other fields included one each in economics and writing and rhetoric. We were surprised that of the 22 authors, 10 authors' affiliations, (or 45%) were unknown. Workplace literacy was the only topic category where "unknown" was the most common affiliation, perhaps reflecting the nature of the journals that commonly publish workplace literacy topics. Over a quarter of the sources (4 out of 14, or 29%) had no education or literacy expertise among the authors.

Family Literacy

The eight sources on the topic of family literacy represented 12 authors. Eight of these authors were in general education (6, or 50%) or literacy education (2, or 25%), while four authors' affiliations (25%) were unknown. Three sources did not indicate author affiliations, most likely due to the nature of the journals in which this topic was published. All of the remaining sources included at least one education or literacy expert. Unlike other topics, all of the sources with known authorship were written by scholars of education. This finding may be due to the fact that the majority of family literacy scholarship tends to focus on children in a family rather than adult literacy; this is something that family literacy and adult literacy researchers may need to attend more to.

Assessment

Our analysis included 26 sources, representing 78 authors, on the topic of assessment. This scholarship occurred in a variety of fields, with healthcare (27 authors, or 35%) and statisticians, independent researchers, and government authors (23 authors, or 29%) being most common. Other fields included fewer than 10 authors; six authors in literacy education, five in general education, four in agriculture, three in psychology or educational psychology, two in human resources and workforce development, and one in economics. Only five authors' affiliations were unknown, and nine of the 26 sources (35%) included no literacy or education expert.

Theory and Policy

Six authors wrote about FL theory; three of these were in general education, two were in literacy education, and one was a statistician. The policy sources represented 14 authors; six in general education fields, three in literacy education, two from statistics or government agencies, two in administrative leadership, and one in Africana studies. All theory sources, and all but two policy sources, included at least one education or literacy expert as an author. Thus, policy and the limited theory sources emerge from educational experts. One surprise was that only two of the policy authors were affiliated with governmental agencies.

Discussion

Literacy is an applied phenomenon as people practice literacy in order to attain goals in different domains of their lives. The burgeoning interest in FL among non-literacy scholars shows that other fields recognize the importance of adult literacy. This is great news! Less encouraging, however, is the finding that one-third of our sources included no literacy or education expertise among the authorship, although this differed widely across applied contexts. Lack of literacy expertise was particularly glaring in the fields of health literacy and assessment, while family literacy was almost entirely dominated by literacy researchers.

We mention here that we recognize a limitation of our study. Our analysis was based on the broad institution as well as the department or division of employment. This does not necessarily reflect the educational background of the authors; there may be education or literacy experts working in various fields. Without further inquiry to the authors' training and expertise, our findings report the assumption that their training is most associated with their current placement. That said, even if our findings are estimates and the education/literacy expertise is higher than accounted for, we notice a need for greater collaboration.

As it currently appears, multidisciplinary research in functional literacy is being conducted, which keeps the assumptions, theories, and tools of health literacy, workplace literacy, family literacy and more within each discipline. Scholars appear to be working in their own isolated disciplinary towers, perhaps contributing to disparities of literacy definitions, conceptualizations, and theories. Such disciplinary isolation, however, likely has stunted the development of our knowledge of literacy, particularly as applied in context(s). Our findings raise important implications about who is considering and thus defining FL.

One major implication is that functional literacy has significant consequences for adults' lives, and our work matters not only in educational settings, but also in families, communities, workplaces, health care settings, and other life contexts. For example, individuals with low literacy have difficulty following directions for prescriptions or medical treatment (Mikulecky, Smith-Burke, & Beatty; Parker & Schwartzberg; Witte). Also, adults with low literacy levels are more likely to be un- or under-employed, earn lower salaries when they are employed, or require public assistance (Kutner et al., 2007). If we view literacy as a multidimensional phenomenon that has cognitive, sociocultural, and critical aspects, then we need to have research teams that reflect all those aspects. Similarly, because literacy/education are applied fields, we need to have research teams that reflect expertise in theory, research, and applied work.

Another implication is that FL is a field ripe for collaboration across disciplines, and literacy researchers may need to more actively reach out to other fields. For example, literacy researchers could help health care researchers better theorize their construct of functional health literacy. Individuals do not possess all the expertise needed to solve problems (Lakhani et al.). Collaboration is a two-way street, and literacy scholars can gain additional theoretical perspectives and methodological approaches from other disciplines and fields. For example, Schneider's (2007) work comes from the field of English, and his historical analysis represents essentially the only thorough consideration of the role of citizenship in FL. Because literacy researchers have much to offer and to gain from cross-disciplinary collaborations, they should be proactive in seeking and developing these collaborations.

We encourage the functional literacy research community at large to begin moving from individual practice to collaborative community through a three-phase process (Siedlok, Hibbert, & Sillince). The first phase, practices of inquiry, is exploratory for individuals to decide if they want to proceed with further collaboration. In this phase, individuals engage in risk taking, exploring, seeking opportunities, and searching for connections with others. Individuals realize there are risks such as potential failure or slower progress, as well as getting out of one's comfort zone. Willingness to expose oneself and entertain new ideas occurs in the exploring phase. Seeking opportunities transpires when an individual looks for a collaborative group without any clear intention or goal. Once a goal and project have been identified, individuals may search for connections with other research partners. Therefore, in this phase, collaborative opportunities may arise serendipitously or purposefully. The second phase is practices of engagement. This "practicing together" includes engaging and accommodating to investigate how ideologies and tools can mesh so collaborators can work together. Then the researchers start to find a focus and build the collaboration. During this phase, the researchers amalgamate and negotiate so all participants are equal. This second phase is a developing stage where genuine collaborations happen as a result of rapport, purposefulness, and synergy. The final phase is practices of enactment. These community-based practices involve nurturing of interpersonal relationships, maintaining procedural justice to recognize all contributions, and brokering connections to ensure that connections fully function as collaborations. If there is any disengagement by participants a group may dissolve. The group may also socialize new participants. The goal is to establish a nurturing, shared understanding and purpose that results in a fully functional, substantially connected team of researchers who sustain their work.

In her 2015 presidential address to the Literacy Research Association, Janice Almasi called upon literacy educators to cross boundaries and engage with others from various fields. Along with Almasi, we advocate for more interdisciplinary research. Let's make interdisciplinary research the standard rather than the exception (Aboelela et al.). Society at large and the adult literacy community, in particular, will benefit from true, collaborative, interdisciplinary partnerships.

Works Cited

Aboelela, Sally W., et al. "Defining Interdisciplinary Research: Conclusions from a Critical Review of the Literature." *Health Services Research* 42.1 (2007): 329-346. Print.

Adkins, Natalie R., and Canan Corus. "Health Literacy for Improved Health Outcomes: Effective Capital in the Marketplace." *Journal of Consumer Affairs* 43.2 (2009): 199-222. Print.

Almasi, Janice. "Crossing Boundaries in Literacy Research: Challenges and Opportunities." Literacy Research Association Conference. Carlsbad, CA. 02 December 2015. Presidential Address.

Amstutz, Donna D., and Vanessa Sheared. "The Crisis in Adult Basic Education." *Education and Urban Society* 32.2 (2000): 155-166. Print.

Askov, Eunice. "Workplace Literacy: Evaluation of the Three Model Programs." *Adult Basic Education* 10.2 (2000): 100-108. Print.

Baer, Justin, et al. "Basic Reading Skills and the Literacy of America's Least Literate Adults: Results from the 2003 National Assessment of Adult Literacy (NAAL) Supplemental Studies. NCES 2009-481." *National Center for Education Statistics* (2009). Print.

Baker, David W., et al. "Functional Health Literacy and the Risk of Hospital Admission Among Medicare Managed Care Enrollees." *American Journal of Public Health* 92.8 (2002): 1278-1283. Print.

Bates, Reid, and Elwood F. Holton. "Linking Workplace Literacy Skills and Transfer System Perceptions." *Human Resource Development Quarterly* 15.2 (2004): 153-170.

Bauske, Ellen M., et al. "Use of Pictorial Evaluations to Measure Knowledge Gained by Hispanic Landscape Workers Receiving Safety Training." *Journal of Extension* 51.5 (2013). Retrieved from http://www.joe.org/joe/2013october/rb3.php

Bennett, Ian M., et al. "The Contribution of Health Literacy to Disparities in Self-Rated Health Status and Preventive Health Behaviors in Older Adults." *Annals of Family Medicine* 7.3 (2009): 204-211.

Benson, Sheila. "Negotiating Literacy Identity in the Face of Perceived Illiteracy: What Counts as Being Literate as an Adult and Who Decides?" *Adult Basic Education & Literacy Journal* 4.3 (2010): 131-139.

Berkman, Nancy D., Terry C. Davis, and Lauren McCormack. "Health Literacy: What Is It?" *Journal of Health Communication* 15.S2 (2010): 9-19.

Bernardo, Allan B. I. "On Defining and Developing Literacy Across Communities." *International Review of Education* 46.5 (2000): 455-465.

Binder, Katherine S., et al. "Dynamic Indicators of Basic Early Literacy Skills: An Effective Tool To Assess Adult Literacy Students?" *Adult Basic Education & Literacy Journal* 5.3 (2011): 150-160.

Binder, Katherine S., and Cheryl S. Lee. "Reader Profiles For Adults With Low Literacy Skills: A Quest To Find Resilient Readers." *Journal of Research & Practice for Adult Literacy, Secondary & Basic Education* 1.2 (2012): 78-90.

Boudard, Emmanuel, and Stan Jones. "The IALS Approach To Defining and Measuring Literacy Skills." *International Journal of Educational Research* 39.3 (2003): 191-204. Print.

Castleton, Geraldine. "Workplace Literacy as a Contested Site of Educational Activity." *Journal of Adolescent & Adult Literacy* 45. 7 (2002): 556-566. Print.

Chesser, Amy, et al. "Health Literacy Assessment of the STOFHLA: Paper Versus Electronic Administration Continuation Study." *Health Education & Behavior* 41.1 (2014): 19-24. Print.

Chisolm, Denna J., and Lindsay Buchanan. "Measuring Adolescent Functional Health Literacy: A Pilot Validation of the Test of Functional Health Literacy in Adults." *Journal of Adolescent Health* 41.3 (2007): 312-314. doi:10.1016/j.jadohealth.2007.04.015

Cohen, Dale J., and Jessica L. Snowden. "The Relations between Document Familiarity, Frequency, and Prevalence and Document Literacy Performance Among Adult Readers." *Reading Research Quarterly* 43.1 (2008): 9-26. Print.

Colbert, Alison M., Susan M. Sereika, and Judith A. Erlen. "Functional Health Literacy, Medication-Taking Self-Efficacy and Adherence to Antiretroviral Therapy." *Journal of Advanced Nursing* 69.2 (2013): 295-304. doi:10.1111/j.1365-2648.2012.06007.x

Collin, Ross, and Michael W. Apple. "Schooling, Literacies and Biopolitics in the Global Age." *Discourse: Studies in the Cultural Politics of Education* 28.4 (2007): 433-454. Print.

Compton-Lilly, Catherine. "Disparate Reading Identities of Adult Students in one GED Program." *Adult Basic Education & Literacy Journal* 3.1 (2009): 34-43. Print.

Compton-Lilly, Catherine, Rebecca Rogers, and Tisha Y. Lewis. "Analyzing Epistemological Considerations Related to Diversity: An Integrative Critical Literature Review of Family Literacy Scholarship." *Reading Research Quarterly* 47.1 (2012): 33-60. Print.

Craig, Judith C. "The Missing Link between School and Work: Knowing the Demands of the Workplace." *English Journal* 91.2 (2001): 46-50. Print.

Cuban, Sondra. "Following the Physician's Recommendations Faithfully and Accurately: Functional Health Literacy, Compliance, and the Knowledge-Based Economy." *Journal for Critical Education Policy Studies* 4.2 (2006): 220-243. Print.

Darcovich, Nancy. "The Measurement of Adult Literacy in Theory and in Practice." *International Review of Education* 46.5 (2000): 367-376. Print.

De Castell, Suzanne, A. Luke, and D. MacLennan. "On Defining Literacy." *Canadian Journal of Education* 6.3 (1981): 7-18. doi: 10.2307/1494652

Diehl, Sandra J. "Health Literacy Education within Adult Literacy Instruction." *New Directions for Adult & Continuing Education* 130 (2011): 29-41. Print.

Druine, Nathalie, and Danny Wildemeersch. "The Vocational Turn in Adult Literacy Education and the Impact of the International Adult Literacy Survey." *International Review of Education* 46.5 (2000): 391-405. Print.

Falk, Ian. "The Future of Work and the Work of the Future." *Journal of Adolescent & Adult Literacy* 44.6 (2001): 566-571. Print.

Fisher, James C., and Larry G. Martin. "The Welfare-To-Work Transition in the United States: Implications for Work-Related Learning." *International Review of Education* 46.6 (2000): 529-544. Print.

Foulk, David, Pamela Carroll, and Susan N. Wood. "Addressing Health Literacy: A Description of the Intersection of Functional Literacy and Health Care." *American Journal of Health Studies*, 17.1 (2001): 7-14. Print.

Freire, Paul. *The Paulo Freire Reader.* Ed. A. Freire and D. Macedo. New York: Continuum, 2001.

Gee, James. "Discourse and Sociocultural Studies in Reading." *Handbook on reading research, volume III*. Ed. M.L. Kamil, P.B. Mosenthal, P.D. Pearson, and R. Barr. London: Routledge, 2000. 195-208.

Golbeck, Amanda L., et al. "Health Literacy and Adult Basic Education Assessments." *Adult Basic Education* 15.3 (2005): 151-168.

_____. "Promoting Health Literacy Through GED Testing." *Adult Basic Education and Literacy Journal* 4.1 (2010): 13-23. Print.

Greenberg, Daphne. "Adult Literacy: The State of the Field." *Perspectives on Language & Literacy* 39.2 (2013): 9-11. Print.

Greenberg, Daphne, et al. "Measuring Adult Literacy Students' Reading Skills Using the Gray Oral Reading Test." *Annals of Dyslexia* 59.2 (2009): 133-149. Print.

_____. "Testing Adult Basic Education Students For Reading Ability and Progress: How Many Tests to Administer?" *Adult Basic Education & Literacy Journal* 4.2 (2010): 96-103. Print.

Guadalupe, Cesar, and Manuel Cardoso. "Measuring the Continuum of Literacy Skills among Adults: Educational Testing and the LAMP Experience." *International Review of Education* 57.1 (2011): 199-217. doi: 10.1007/s11159-011-9203-2

Hamilton, Mary, and David Barton. "The International Adult Literacy Survey: What Does It Really Measure?" *International Review of Education* 46.5 (2000): 377-389. Print.

Hannon, Peter. "Rhetoric and Research in Family Literacy." *British Educational Research Journal* 26.1 (2000): 121-38. Print.

Hautecoeur, Jean-Paul. "Editorial Introduction: Literacy in the Age of Information: Knowledge, Power or Domination?" *International Review of Education* 46.5 (2000): 357-365. Print.

Hepburn, Millie. "Health Literacy, Conceptual Analysis for Disease Prevention." *International Journal of Collaborative Research on Internal Medicine & Public Health* 4.3 (2012): 228-238. Print.

Huber, Jeffrey T., Robert M. Shapiro II, and Mary L. Gillaspy. "Top Down Versus Bottom Up: The Social Construction of the Health Literacy Movement." *The Library Quarterly* 82.4 (2012): 429-451. Print.

Hull, Glynda, and Katherine Schultz. "Literacy and Learning Out of School: A Review of Theory and Research." *Review of Educational Research* 71.4 (2001): 575-611. Print.

Kazemek, Francis E. ""Now is the time to evaluate our lives": The Elderly as a Touchstone for Adult Literacy Education." *Adult Basic Education* 13.2 (2003): 67-80. Retrieved from http://search.proquest.com/docview/227578282?accountid=14556

Kirsch, Irwin S. "The Framework Used in Developing and Interpreting the International Adult Literacy Survey." *European Journal of Psychology of Education* 16.3 (2001): 335-361. Print.

Kohler, Maxie P., and Gary L. Sapp. "Implementation of the "PDQ—Building Skills for Using Print" Workplace Literacy Program for High-Risk Women: A New Approach." *Adult Basic Education* 10.1 (2000): 39-48. Print.

Kutner, Mark, et al. "Literacy in Everyday Life: Results from the 2003 National Assessment of Adult Literacy." *National Center For Education Statistics* 490 (2007). Print.

_____. "The health literacy of America's adults: Results from the 2003 National Assessment of Adult Literacy." *National Center for Education Statistics* 483 (2006). Print.

Laanan, Frankie S., and Elizabeth M. Cox. "Political and Structural Divide: An Holistic Approach to Family Literacy Programs at Community Colleges." *Community College Journal of Research and Practice* 30.4 (2006): 359-372. Print.

Lakhani, Jahan, Karen Benzies, and K. Alix Hayden. "Attributes of Interdisciplinary Research Teams: A Comprehensive Review of the Literature." *Clinical and Investigative Medicine* 35.5 (2012): E260-E265. Print.

Lewis, Cynthia, Patricia Enciso, and Elizabeth B. Moje. *Reframing Sociocultural Research on Literacy: Identity, Agency, and Power.* Mahwah, NJ: Lawrence Erlbaum Associates, 2007a. Print.

Liddicoat, Anthony J. "Language Planning for Literacy: Issues and Implications." *Current Issues in Language Planning* 5.1 (2004): 1-17. Print.

Lynch, Jacueline. "Print Literacy Engagement of Parents from Low-Income Backgrounds: Implications for Adult and Family Literacy Programs." *Journal of Adolescent and Adult Literacy* 52.6 (2009): 509-521. Print.

Manzo, Anthony V. "Literacy Crisis or Cambrian Period? Theory, Practice, and Public Policy implications." *Journal of Adolescent & Adult Literacy* 46.8 (2003): 654-661. Print.

Mellard, Daryl, Emily Fall, and Kari L. Woods. "A Path Analysis of Reading Comprehension for Adults With Low Literacy." *Journal of Learning Disabilities* 43.2 (2010): 154-165. Print.

Mellard, Daryl, Margaret B. Patterson, and Sara Prewett. "Reading Practices among Adult Education Participants." *Reading Research Quarterly* 42.2 (2007): 188-213. Print.

Mellard, Daryl, Kari Woods, and Deana Desa. "Literacy and Numeracy among Job Corps Students: Opportunities for Targeted Academic Infusion in CTE." *Career & Technical Education Research* 37.2 (2012): 141-156. Print.

Mellard, Daryl, Kari Woods, and Emily Fall. "Assessment and Instruction of Oral Reading Fluency among adults with low literacy." *Adult Basic Education & Literacy Journal* 5.1 (2011): 3-14. Print.

Mikulecky, Larry, Trika Smith-Burke, and Jeanine Beatty. "Adult Literacy Research in 2006: Where Did It Appear, What Methodologies Were Used, and What Did It Say? *Adult Basic Education & Literacy Journal* 3.2 (2009): 67-76. Print.

Mohadjer, Leyla, et al. "National assessment of adult literacy: Indirect county and state estimates of the percentage of adults at the lowest literacy level for 1992 and 2003." *National Center for Education Statistics* 482 (2009). Print.

Morrow, Dan, et al. "Correlates of Health Literacy in Patients with Chronic Heart Failure." *Gerontologist* 46.5 (2006): 669-676. Print.

"National Adult Literacy Survey." *National Center for Education Statistics*, (1992).

"National Assessment of Adult Literacy." *National Center for Education Statistics*, (2003). Retrieved from http://nces.ed.gov/NAAL/fr_definition.asp

National Literacy Act. Pub. Law, 102-73 (25 Jul. 1991).

Ntiri, Daphne W. "Toward a Functional and Culturally Salient Definition of Literacy." *Adult Basic Education and Literacy Journal* 3.2 (2009): 97-104. Print.

OECD. "Literacy in the information age: Final report of the International Adult Literacy Survey." Paris: OECD, (2000). Retrieved from http://www.oecd.org/edu/skills-beyond-school/41529765.pdf

Olson, Kristen, et al. "The Self-Assessed Literacy Index: Reliability and Validity." *Social Science Research* 40.5 (2011): 1465-1476. Print.

Ozanne, Julie L., Natalie R. Adkins, and Jennifer A. Sandlin. "Shopping (for) Power: How Adult Literacy learners negotiate the marketplace." *Adult Education Quarterly* 55.4 (2005): 251-268. Print.

Parker, Ruth M., and Joanne G. Schwartzberg. "What Patients Do-And Don't-Understand." *Postgraduate Medicine* 109.5 (2001): 13-16. Print.

Pennell, Michael. ""If knowledge is power, you're about to become very powerful": Literacy and Labor Market Intermediaries in Postindustrial America." *College Composition and Communication* 58.3 (2007): 345-384. Print.

Perry, Kristen H. "Genres, Contexts, and Literacy Practices: Literacy Brokering among Sudanese Refugee Families." *Reading Research Quarterly* 44.3 (2009): 256-276. Print.

———. "What Is Literacy? —A Critical Overview of Sociocultural Perspectives." *Journal of Language and Literacy Education* 8.1 (2012): 50-71.Print.

Prins, Esther, and Ramazan Gungor. "Family Literacy Funding Reductions and Work-First Welfare Policies: Adaptations and Consequences in Family Literacy Programs." *Adult Basic Education and Literacy Journal* 5.1 (2011): 15-25. Print.

Purcell-Gates, Victoria, et al. "Impact of Authentic Adult Literacy Instruction on Adult Literacy Practices." *Reading Research Quarterly* 37.1 (2002): 70-92. Print.

Quigley, B. Allan. "Living in the Feudalism of Adult Basic and Literacy Education: Can We Negotiate a Literacy Democracy?" *New Directions for Adult & Continuing Education* 91 (2001): 55-62. Print.

Robinson, Petra A. "Literacy Engagement and Parental Development through Even Start Family Literacy Participation." *Journal of Research and Practice for Adult Literacy, Secondary, and Basic Education* 1.1 (2012): 19-29. Print.

Rogers, Rebecca. "Storied selves: A Critical Discourse Analysis of Adult Learners' Literate Lives." *Reading Research Quarterly* 39.3 (2004): 272-305. Print.

Rogers, Rebecca, and Inda Schaenen. "Critical Discourse Analysis in Literacy Education: A Review of the Literature." *Reading Research Quarterly* 49.1 (2013): 121-143.

Rose, Mike. "Words in Action: Rethinking Workplace Literacy." *Research in the Teaching of English* 38.1 (2003): 125-128. Print.

Rudd, Rima E. "Health Literacy Skills of U.S. Adults." *American Journal of Health Behavior* 31 (2007): S8-S-18. Print.

Schneider, Stephen. "The Sea Island Citizenship Schools: Literacy, Community Organization, and the Civil Rights Movement." *College English* 70.2 (2007): 144-167. Print.

Selber, Stuart A. "Reimagining the Functional Side of Computer Literacy." *College Composition and Communication* 55.3 (2004): 470-503. Print.

Sheehan-Holt, Janet K., and M. Cecil Smith. "Does Basic Skills Education Affect Adults' Literacy Proficiencies and Reading Practices?" *Reading Research Quarterly* 35.2 (2000): 226-243. Print.

Siedlok, Frank, Paul Hibbert, and John Sillince. "From Practice to Collaborative Community in Interdisciplinary Research Contexts." *Research Policy* 44 (2015): 96-107. Print.

Smith, M. Cecil. "The Real-World Reading Practices of Adults." *Journal of Literacy Research* 32.1 (2000): 25-52. Print.

Smith, M. Cecil, et al. "What Will Be the Demands of Literacy in the Workplace in the Next Millennium?" *Reading Research Quarterly* 35.3 (2000): 378-83. Print.

St. Clair, Ralf, and Jennifer A. Sandlin. "Incompetence and Intrusion: On the Metaphorical Use of Illiteracy in the U.S. Political Discourse." *Adult Basic Education* 14.1 (2004): 45-59. Print.

Staudinger, Ursula M. "Towards Truly Interdisciplinary Research on Human Development." *Research in Human Development* 12.3-4 (2015): 335-341. Print.

Sum, Andrew. "Forces Changing Our Nation's Future: The Comparative Performance of U.S. Adults and Youth On International Literacy Assessments, the Importance of Literacy/Numeracy Proficiencies for Labor Market Success, and the Projected Outlook for Literacy Proficiencies of U.S. Adults." *National Commission on Adult Literacy (NJ1)*, 2007. Retrieved from http://caalusa.org/forceschangingfuture.pdf

Tracey, Diane, Alex Storer, and Sohrob Kazerounian. "Cognitive Processing Perspectives on the New Literacies." *The new literacies: Multiple perspectives on research and practice*. Ed. E.A. Baker. 2010. 106-130. Print.

Townsend, Tony, John Pisapia, and Jamila Razzaq. "Fostering Interdisciplinary Research in Universities: A Case Study of Leadership, Alignment and Support." *Studies in Higher Education* 40.4 (2015): 658-675. Print.

UNESCO. "Literacy in Asia: A Continuing Challenge." *Report of the UNESCO Regional Experts Meeting on Literacy in Asia (Bangkok, 22–28 November 1977).* Bangkok: UNESCO Regional Office for Education in Asia and Oceania., 1978. Retrieved from http://www.uis.unesco.org/Library/Documents/gmr06-en.pdf

Valdivielso, Sofia. "Functional Literacy, Functional Illiteracy: The Focus of an Ongoing Social Debate." *Convergence* 39.2/3 (2006): 123-129. Print.

_____. "The Collective That Didn't Quite Collect: Reflections on the IALS." *International Review of Education* 46.5 (2000): 419-4314. Print.

Venezky, Richard L. "The origins of the present-day chasm between adult literacy needs and school literacy instruction." *Scientific Studies of Reading* 4.1 (2000): 19-39. Print.

Viswanathan, Madhubalan, Jose A. Rosa, and James E. Harris. "Decision Making and Coping of Functionally Illiterate Consumers and Some Implications for Marketing Management." *Journal of Marketing* 69.1 (2005): 15-31. Print.

Wagner, Daniel A. "Adult literacy: Monitoring and Evaluation for Practice and Policy." *International Review of Education* 54.5/6 (2008): 651-672. Print.

Wallendorf, Melanie. "Literally Literacy." *Journal of Consumer Research* 27.4 (2001): 505-511. Print.

White, Sheida. "Mining the Text: 34 Text Features That Can Ease or Obstruct Text Comprehension and Use." *Literacy Research & Instruction* 51.2 (2012): 143-164. Print.

_____. "The Cognitive and Linguistic Demands of Everyday, Functional Literacy Tasks: With Application to an Over-The-Counter Drug Label." *Written Language and Literacy,* 14.2 (2011a): 224-250. doi:10.1075/wll.14.2.03whi

_____. *Understanding Adult Functional Literacy: Connecting Text Features, Task Demands, and Respondent Skills.* New York: Routledge, 2011b. Print.

White, Sheida, and Sally. Dillow. "Key Concepts and Features of the 2003 National Assessment of Adult Literacy." *National Center for Education Statistics* 471 (2005). Print.

Witte, Priscilla G. "Health Literacy: Can We Live Without It?" *Adult Basic Education and Literacy Journal* 4.1 (2010): 3-12. Print.

Wolf, Michael S., et al. "Literacy and Learning in Health Care." *Pediatrics* 124 Supplement 3 (2009): S275-S281. Print.

Author Bios

Donita Shaw is an associate professor of literacy education at Oklahoma State University. Her scholarship focuses on three themes: adult functional literacy, teachers' literacy beliefs solicited through metaphors, and classroom interventions with a focus on alphabetics and word study.

Kristen H. Perry is an associate professor of literacy education at the University of Kentucky. Her work focuses primarily on literacy and culture in diverse communities, investigating everyday home/family and community literacy practices, particularly among immigrant and refugee communities. She also researches educational opportunities with respect to ESL, literacy, and higher education for adult refugees. Perry is the 2012 recipient of the Literacy Research Association's Early Career Achievement award and their 2007 J. Michael Parker Award for research in adult literacy.

Lyudmyla Ivanyuk is a doctoral student in Literacy at the University of Kentucky. Her interests in literacy and culture result from her own experiences as an international student and ESL teacher. She taught English to college students for four years in Ukraine, followed by three years of teaching English to international students at two American universities. Her research focuses on adult writing development among speakers of English as a second language.

Sarah Tham is a PhD Candidate in the literacy program in the Curriculum and Instruction department at the University of Kansas. She is currently working on her dissertation which explores the self-reflection of America Reads tutors who tutor striving readers, using the Korthagen self-reflection model. She is also interested in online learning and the cultural differences involved in it, as well as adolescent literacy, and she continues to work with K-12 striving readers.

Navigating Difficulty in Classroom-Community Outreach Projects

Lauren Rosenberg

Abstract

Sustainability in community engagement projects depends on careful attention to the ways we navigate complex, often challenging relationships with our partners, our students, agencies, and the institutions in which we occupy multiple, sometimes competing roles. This article considers the difficulty inherent in developing and maintaining relationships with the community members who choose to participate in our research. Based on the experiences of three undergraduate students in a community literacy seminar, the author traces the ways these students confront challenges in their projects, arguing for the value of difficulty in community literacy work.

Keywords: difficulty, sustainability, relationships with community partners, community outreach, Building Engaged Infrastructure, undergraduate teaching

Developing and valuing relationships is implicit in the work we do as university-community practitioners who seek greater engagement with people in the settings where we come together. Perhaps the desire to nourish relationships *is* what sparks community literacy workers to want to keep reaching out into seemingly impractical situations and projects not likely to succeed—at least not in manageable, semester-measurable terms. Ultimately, our work is always about relating with people over the ways writing has value in their lives. At one of the Deep Think Tanks I participated in at the inaugural Conference on Community Writing (CCW), we gathered in groups to answer the question: What sustains you professionally in this work? The question bothered me because it encourages narratives of personal fulfillment—as it did in my group: expressions of *I did right, I was a good person, I developed viable relationships*. My own experiences doing community outreach work, and especially doing this work within an institution that nods and approves, yet with little genuine interest in the impact of my or anyone else's projects—except that such work makes the institution look good—is that the question of what sustains you is not easily answered, and when it is answered, the response is not so rosy. Sustainability in community engagement projects depends on careful attention to the ways we navigate complex, often challenging relationships with our partners, our students, agencies, and the institutions in which we occupy multiple, sometimes competing roles.

Sustaining relationships is difficult work, a sometimes-overlooked part of building engaged infrastructure ("Building Engaged Infrastructure" was the theme of the CCW). When I speak of difficulty in working through relationships with community members, I am interested in difficulty as a necessary and productive concept. I am not pointing to the worry or sense of failure that community literacy researchers have investigated in discussions of unsustainability. Paul Feigenbaum, in his keynote address at the CCW, encouraged us to get past the trope of unsustainability that has been popular in conversations since Jessica Restaino and Laurie Cella published *Unsustainable* in 2012 by spinning the focus of community literacy work to look at moments of "pleasant surprise" and wonder in the "unpredictable encounters" we have in our work. Most would agree that looking for the joy in what we do is why we keep doing it. But I want to consider the value of difficulty in negotiating these relationships and why that is the most meaningful challenge we have in community outreach work—perhaps, I'd suggest, what ultimately gives us joy. A key part of building infrastructure is engaging difficulty. Paying attention to difficulty encourages us to see that community relations are fluid, unstable, and constantly changing. By looking at our work as always shifting, we may get a sense of greater sustainability than when we assume some sort of successful, static model that can be applied across contexts. As Eli Goldblatt proposed in his talk at the CCW, for our work to be viable, we should be open to continually revising our definitions.

Cultivating Relationships with Participants in a Community Literacy Seminar

At my university, I teach an undergraduate capstone class on community literacy studies. The class is a yearlong seminar for English majors that concentrates on critical literacy scholarship during the first semester and in which students put a small-scale study of their own design into action during the second semester. By applying what they have read to what they then do, students in the seminar problematize the idea of community and what it means to intervene in settings outside the university based on their experiences. Their interaction with the scholarship, and then their enactment of it, join together social and personal concerns as they confront them through the lens of community literacy studies.

I'm not doing the "writing with" and "writing for" projects that Deans identifies (*Writing Partnerships*), or the work with agencies that has been explored by Steve Parks and Eli Goldblatt in their ongoing collaborations with community partners (Parks; Goldblatt "Alinsky's", *Because*). My course focuses more on understanding *why* and making connections *between* the theories we have studied and the reasons for reaching out into communities. Because students design their own small-scale ethnographic studies, they have to decide what matters and how to examine literacy practices in communities. Their projects range from participant observation in an existing writers group at a senior center to informal conversations with Latino community members as they stand in line to negotiate benefits at a Department of Social Services office.

I have learned from teaching this class that we must be explicit in guiding students in their interactions with community members if they are to develop meaningful relationships that are valuable for all involved. Like Tom Deans, I focus on "how developing good working relationships with their partner organization is a critical part—usually *the* most critical part—of community-based writing" ("Sustainability Deferred" 104). For me, as a teacher of community literacy studies, one of the significant challenges is directing students in their self-designed outreach projects and helping them figure out how to foster relationships with the community members who participate in their research. As Lorelei Blackburn and Ellen Cushman argue in "Assessing Sustainability," emphasizing relationships is the most vital component of community literacy work and the area where we need to concentrate more of our effort as researchers and teachers: "[And] if a methodology for developing relationships is interwoven, then relationship building becomes not just a *component* of the curriculum, but a way of *delivering* curriculum" (163). Unsurprisingly, difficulties arose as students conducted their projects. During the semester when the class was actively engaged in their individual studies, our whole group meetings concentrated on how to gauge delicate social interactions more than on any other topic. Navigating relationships with participants, most of all understanding how to address moments of disconnection, was, as Deans observed, the most significant challenge for students in the class and the central point of our discussions. As a group, we problem solved about what each student in the class might do to make appropriate, ethical, timely decisions while always placing participants' needs first.

Three Snapshots

What follows are snapshots from three students' projects as they addressed challenges in their relationships with community members when they put their objectives for community outreach projects into action. Their examples illustrate why we need to be open to shifting and redefining our methods and recognizing the changeability of the communities in which we engage—as well as the changeability of our students—for this work to be sustainable.

Michelle: Responding to Shifting Conditions

Michelle knew, even before she proposed her study, that she wanted to work with children in a homeless shelter. She was studying to be an elementary school teacher and was therefore interested in a project that involved children writing in an informal site. The questions of why a shelter environment would be the best possible situation and what she expected to do once she got there shaped her study. She did some research on local shelters that house families. Together, she and I met with one of the administrators, a nun who functioned as a kind of gatekeeper of volunteers, and then Michelle continued on her own to consult with the coordinator of educational programs and eventually to create the writing group that she would lead weekly at the shelter. In her finished seminar paper, Michelle reflected on the importance of being flexible as a researcher because she was at a place where conditions were changing all the time:

> The first week I went in, introduced myself, and had them start right away with two prompts that I had prepared. They seemed to rush through it and I felt I did not have enough planned for them. I left feeling very uneasy about how the session went, and I knew I could not continue to do the same type of activity for the remaining weeks. I did not think they would ever feel comfortable with me being there, but I was proved wrong. As I started to alter my writing activities to make them more relatable to the kids, the participants produced more writing, laughed together at meetings, and generally seemed to be enjoying their time. By the fifth week, I even had one of the kids ask me what they would be doing the following week. As they became more comfortable with me being there, I started to feel more like a part of their group, and the results were rewarding. This was a group that had trouble trusting the consistency of people and activities, so once they saw that I was there week after week, the level of comfort increased as did the stability.

Michelle's problem was that children who resided in the shelter expected conditions to change frequently. They were unaccustomed to routine activities. One child was so resistant to participating in the writing group that he wrote the following note: "Dear Michelle, I do not like doing your creative writing because every day I have to go to school every day [sic] and I need to pay attention to me [sic] school work and home work plus I have to walk home every day from school and it is tiering [sic]. Sorry ☹ not to be mean or any thing. I just need to focus on my work." Soon after delivering the note, however, the boy conceded and chose to participate. Michelle tried to model for the children in her writing group consistent focused activity within their temporary home. Administrators at the shelter supported her efforts, but in order for her writing group to succeed, Michelle had to convince the children themselves. This was no easy task, as the note demonstrates, yet as Michelle kept coming to the shelter at the designated time, week after week, the children began to rely on her presence and eventually learned to appreciate her enough to enjoy writing with her.

Jessica: Integrity of Researcher

Jessica, an older student who is a parent and a worker, was intrigued by some of the published scholarship on literacy and social class, and used it to examine her own experiences as a working-class rural woman. Based on Jamie White-Farnham's research on women's heritage literacies, Jessica designed a study of the personal cookbooks that rural working-class women and men create as an aspect of their domestic lives. She spent the summer between semesters developing the project, and she came to me in the fall with a furrowed brow: What was she going to do? Twenty of her acquaintances volunteered to participate. How would she select? Later, when she had winnowed the potential participants to six and the cookbook interviews were in progress, Jessica was confronted with a completely different problem. She described the trouble in a section of her seminar paper that she titled, "Integrity of Recipe":

> As a woman who grew up in rural society, I am a member of that community; however, my education and status of researcher makes me an outsider. As an insider, it could have been easy for me to overlook something, or make assumptions. I needed to make it a priority to really listen to what my participants were saying. I knew the participants in my study very well and anticipated what they were going to say. However, during each interview they said one or two things that really surprised me...
>
> As an outsider, I worried that my participants would freeze up and not offer as much information as they could. I found this to be true when I sat down with my participants. As soon as the tape recorder was turned on the interviews became awkward. My participants became nervous and began to clam up. Most of them began to talk differently, in a more formal tone. A lot of the information that I received from my participants was received after the tape recorder was turned off. Beverly J. Moss discusses some of these aspects of research in her article "Ethnography and Composition: Studying Language at Home." She addresses gaining trust within the community. She also talks about the difficulties that come about when writing up research in a community that you are familiar with. She cautioned about not assuming what participants will say. She also expressed the difficulties about studying people that you know, and not wanting to disappoint them or hurt your feelings when writing about them. This article is a good moral guide as I work through my study.

Jessica's shift in position from longtime acquaintance to a representative of the university who was approaching people with a series of questions and a recording device, came off as a threat to the participants, her lifetime acquaintances, most of who hadn't attended college and suddenly saw their old friend as starkly different from them. Although our class offered her advice, only Jessica could know how best to maintain relationships while encouraging participants to contribute to her study. After a few bad experiences, she decided that she would have to concentrate her attention on balancing between unrecorded—and thus less accurate—interviews or risk intimidating those with whom she wished to engage. There was no easy answer. She walked this tightrope throughout the entire study.

Laurel: Unpredictable Encounters
Laurel had serious problems with access. Initially, she hoped to work with residents at a halfway house for women who were completing their prison sentences. She spent over a month calling and visiting the residence, trying to make contact with the program director. But after a long time of ignoring her calls and visits, the administrator informed Laurel that they were no longer working with volunteers.

Various community literacy researchers have reflected on the project that goes wrong (Paula Mathieu in *Tactics of Hope*; Lisa Mastrangelo in "First Year Composition and Women in Prison"; Blackburn and Cushman in the chapter mentioned above, etc.). One of the terrible outcomes can be that the student is left without a project in the middle of the semester; such was Laurel's plight. But she *had* to have a seminar study, and it *had* to work or she wouldn't graduate, so after a number of other false starts— and great stubbornness on her part—she found an alternative. Laurel situated her study at the Omega House, a residence for adults with HIV/AIDS who are homeless or at risk of homelessness. At first, she was simply relieved to have a place for her research. But in addition to finding a new location, Laurel also had to redesign the project to suit her new population. She had expected to work with prisoners on the "next step" of their rehabilitation, which involved prescribed writing tasks. At Omega House, there was no writing component. So Laurel designed a writing group with the hope that residents would attend. She came prepared with prompts, paper, and pens, yet she was unprepared for the overall interest the residents had in writing. All of the residents participated in her group, and some asked for additional assistance with editing and typing their journal entries, poetry, letters, and stories. Laurel assumed that residents would have difficulty writing; however, she found that they were enthusiastic writers, and that a few of them looked toward writing as a means of self-therapy and personal fulfillment. She reflected on this in a section of her seminar paper titled, "Exhilaration and Revelation":

> Over the course of the last few months that I spent at Omega House, I realized how much I learned about the residents in such a short period of time. They had all been kind enough to join my weekly writing group and to give me samples of the writing that they wrote with me every Thursday night. I had noticed multiple patterns in terms of content. The most common content themes are related to prior drug addiction, fears and regrets, and a longing for missed family and friends. The residents appeared to have a strong desire to share their writing with me. At the end of each weekly writing activity, they persuaded me to keep their work. What I found most rewarding and shocking was when the residents began to write about topics other than my drafted prompts. A few of them also brought in different pieces of writing that they had been working on. Although I am not aware of their educational backgrounds, one thing is for sure, many of them are quite literate, and they turn to writing to reflect and figure things out.

Laurel could not have predicted that the participants in her writing group would be so willing to write or that they would be so eager to share their texts. What began as a daunting situation transformed into one of openness and productivity as participants created new writing and revised older pieces for Laurel, their new audience.

Committing to Difficulty

Eventually, all of the projects succeeded, and each of the fifteen students in class gained appropriate closure with participating individuals and agencies. Every situation was different, however, and many relationships were complicated to the extent that all relationships and situations are varied and complex. While some community literacy workers have bemoaned such difficulty, calling it failure or "unsustainability," I found, along with my students, that these are precisely the moments that are most valuable because they offer opportunities in which significant learning occurs. These are the "unpredictable encounters" that Feigenbaum refers to as possibility, as sustainability.

But I find it necessary to continue viewing instances of difficulty as they are, as moments that threaten a student's and/or a participant's sense of stability. In order to work through the challenges, students and their community partners need to pay attention to instability as an opportunity to reconfigure their community partner relationships. The three snapshots demonstrate how negotiating difficulty can lead to a more engaged relationship: How could Michelle develop and maintain trust? How could Jessica hope to conduct ethical research with the recorder off? How could Laurel listen to participants' accounts, talk with them, and record their words as they wished them to be documented? Michelle, Jessica, and Laurel completed their projects knowing that, along with their participants, they had created something together. They had invested mutually in this work.

None of these relationships could have succeeded within a single model of a community partner relationship. Michelle, Jessica, and Laurel's experiences suggest that we need a more fluid model for how to interact in outreach projects. Moments of difficulty can be heavy with frustration and anxiety for all involved; yet, they contain opportunities for collaboration, for problem solving, both in and outside of the classroom. In this way, difficulty can yield to greater meaning. That is when the critical self and social examination occurs. Having to work through difficulty was, in the end, what made the projects valuable and meaningful.

Works Cited

Blackburn, Lorelei and Ellen Cushman, "Assessing Sustainability: The Class That Went Terribly Wrong." *Unsustainable.* Print.

Deans, Thomas. *Writing Partnerships: Service-Learning in Composition.* Urbana: NCTE, 2000. Print.

_____. "Sustainability Deferred: The Conflicting Logics of Career Advancement and Community Engagement" *Unsustainable.* 101-111. Print.

Feigenbaum, Paul. "Itinerant Networks of a (Still) Frustrated Idealist: Or, Can (and Should) Community Literacy Practitioners Move from Serendipitous Encounters to Formal Infrastructures?" Conference on Community Writing, University of Colorado, Boulder, CO. 15 Oct. 2015. Keynote speech.

Goldblatt, Eli. "Alinsky's Reveille: A Community-Organizing Model of Neighborhood-Based Literacy Projects." *College English.* 67.3 (2005): 274-294. Print.

_____. *Because We Live Here: Sponsoring Literacy Beyond the Curriculum.* Cresskill, NJ: Hampton P, 2007. Print.

_____. "How to LEARN & Why We Care." Conference on Community Writing, University of Colorado, Boulder, CO. 16 Oct. 2015. Keynote speech.

Mastrangelo, Lisa. "First Year Composition and Women in Prison: Service-Based Writing and Community Action." *Reflections: A Journal of Public Rhetoric, Civic Writing, and Service Learning.* 4.1 (2004). Print.

Mathieu, Paula. *Tactics of Hope: The Public Turn in English Composition.* Portsmouth, NH: Boynton/Cook, 2005. Print.

Parks, Stephen. *Gravyland: Writing Beyond the Curriculum in the City of Brotherly Love.* Syracuse: Syracuse UP, 2010. Print.

Restaino, Jessica and Laurie JC Cella, *Unsustainable: Re-imagining Community Literacy, Public Writing, Service-Learning and the University.* Lanham, MD: Lexington Books, 2013. Print.

Thank you to all the students in the 2014 Community Literacy Studies seminar at Eastern Connecticut State University who gave permission for their experiences and work to be mentioned in this paper and especially to those whose writing is excerpted here: Michelle Hoetjes, Laurel Payzant, and Jessica Wainman.

Author Bio

Lauren Rosenberg is the author of *The Desire for Literacy: Writing in the Lives of Adult Learners*, CCCC/NCTE Studies in Writing and Rhetoric series, 2015. Rosenberg's literacy research extends from the study of adult learners in her book to a current project on the writing practices of military personnel while in service in relation to the practices they develop as university students and faculty. Her writing on literacy issues has appeared in *Community Literacy Journal* and *Reflections, A Journal of Public Rhetoric, Civic Writing, and Service Learning*. She has also co-authored a number of book chapters and articles on feminist rhetorics and on writing program administration. At her home institution, New Mexico State University, Rosenberg teaches courses in literacy studies and composition theory. She is director of NMSU's writing program and associate department head in English. From 2006–2016 she was on the faculty at Eastern Connecticut State University.

Book & New Media Reviews

Saul Hernandez, Assistant Editor
Georgia College and State University

From the Book & New Media Review Editor's Desk

Jessica Shumake, University of Arizona

As a journalist for my college newspaper, I frequently found myself tasked to initiate conversations with people attending campus events. I recall an assignment to write a story about residence hall move-in day. As I stood in a busy corridor, a Pentax camera strap around my neck, I attempted to initiate conversations with housing staff, parents, and new students as they carried cardboard boxes, plastic grocery bags, and rolled aluminum dollies. Few people wanted to talk with a student reporter on move-in day, though nearly all accepted the offer of an extra pair of hands to carry a load of stuff. After twenty minutes spent hesitating, I worked up the courage to ask a senior residence life advisor a question. Without a hint of irony, I ask if he had any "profound" thoughts to share with *Captain's Log* readers regarding being an RA. He looked at me, blinked a few times, and said "profound" with a rising intonation and an abrupt exhalation of air.

Had I asked him to tell me a story about a day he felt challenged as an RA, about his biggest pet peeve, or about his hall's bulletin board design, the conversation may have gone in a useful direction. Instead, he turned away. With this misstep, the conversation ended before it ever really began: "move along, aspiring journalist, there's nothing 'profound' here worth discussing and people have real work to do." Even as a green reporter, I understood that a good quote, from the right source, is the lifeblood of a story worth reading. If no one I spoke with had anything substantial to say, there was no story. What I struggled with most as a reporter assigned to write a story about move-in day was my own confidence in drawing out strangers' stories. In fact, I did not write the student move-in article assigned to me and instead covered a soccer game as a photographer. As I reflect on the "profoundest" article I never wrote, it is the ordinariness of the situation that I turn over in my mind over twenty years later.

As I read the reviews assembled in this issue, I am inspired by the firmness of purpose I know to be required in putting one's words into the world. Christopher M. Brown's review of Kelly Ritter's *Reframing the Subject* offers significant insight into post-WWII Coronet instructional films as proto-MOOCs (massively open online courses). Brown's review explores how these films addressed increasing enrollment and college access demands placed on educators due to the GI Bill. For large numbers of students, these films replaced "meaningful teacher-student interaction with one-way regurgitation of tasks modeled on-screen." Educational access narratives that require literacy instruction to be packaged as a commodity, through mass-delivery systems, according to Brown's reading of Ritter, are more likely to be impediments to "social and economic mobility" than the salve they profess to be.

Sandra Shattuck deploys a rhetoric of slowness and explores how our sense of time changes in the face our culture's obsession with speed in her review of Berg and Seeber's *The Slow Professor*. Rachel Buck's review of *Composition in the Age of Austerity* likewise explores labor and knowledge-building practices in writing studies and the impact of an increasingly stark fiscal landscape on the literacy needs and goals of our local communities. In Madelyn Pawlowski's review of *Grassroots Literacies*, she examines sexual literacy, collective action, and the normative narrative arcs through which LGBT and queer subjects navigate a politics of invisibility and becoming in Turkey. Sally Benson's review of *The Desire for Literacy* explores the unarticulated values and assumptions that constitute what literacy means for adults who seek to further their literacy learning in domains outside of formal school contexts. Eric A. House's review of *Freedom Writing* is keenly attentive to the function spirituality, music, and singing played in grassroots literacy education and civil rights activism for black people at the Sea Island Citizenship School in South Carolina. All of these reviews, and the writers who composed them, follow in the tradition of writing as a communal endeavor that is at its best when it is realized on the page. All of these reviews reflect on how we come to understand literacy and the complex frameworks that keep many of us, in reviewer Sally Benson's words, "hush-mouthed" or even render us silent.

Reframing the Subject:
Postwar Instructional Film and Class-Conscious Literacies

Kelly Ritter
Pittsburgh: U of Pittsburgh Press, 2015. 368 pp.

Reviewed by Christopher M. Brown
University of Arizona

In *Reframing the Subject*, Kelly Ritter offers a rigorous and incisive account of the use of instructional films, a subset of "mental hygiene" films, in literacy education following World War II. This book will appeal to an array of scholars and teachers, including those interested in histories of literacy education, the role of social class in US education, and the use of technology in writing instruction. In an era of rapid material and economic growth, instructional films capitalized on an emerging medium to train students in foundational principles of speaking and writing, social conduct, and democratic citizenship. Ritter argues that the narratives and lessons presented in these films nurtured the myth of literacy as a path to social mobility, while simultaneously instructing students to retain the attitudes and behaviors of their socioeconomic classes. The book includes chapters on cultural and curricular developments that set the foundation for instructional film's use in secondary and postsecondary schools, analyses of the pedagogical and class-based values implicit in specific films, and connections between the instructional film's legacy and current iterations of online literacy instruction in higher education. While these films may be dismissed as remnants of a bygone era, Ritter makes a compelling case that the attitudes that established their appeal remain an intrinsic part of our pedagogies today. In that sense, the book issues a timely call for educators to reconsider the connections between our methods of classroom instruction and the material realities of students' lives.

Ritter observes that the promise of higher education, as a pathway to the comfort and security of a middle-class lifestyle, emerged at the end of World War II. At this time, economic and material advances, along with government measures like the GI Bill, made it possible for increasing numbers of Americans to attend college. In the decades that followed, Ritter argues, the myth of social uplift through education was inculcated through literacy instruction at the secondary and postsecondary levels, with harmful consequences for students. One prominent vehicle of this myth was the instructional film, which offered streamlined instruction in literacy-based values and practices that students would need for academic and professional success. At the same time, the films employed visual, verbal, and narrative cues to situate this instruction in the wider context of lessons in social etiquette, morality, and other behaviors representative of an idealized middle class. Consequently, only those students who had acquired prior knowledge of these behaviors, usually in their home communities, benefitted from such lessons. Students who lacked such knowledge were unable to identify with the characters and scenarios presented on screen, reinforcing their status as outsiders to middle-class culture and discouraging their economic mobility. "The films are thus a paradox," writes Ritter, "wherein lessons are presented as universal 'truths' but only to those who already know and believe those truths as part of their existing socioeconomic identities" (33). Through this paradox, the postwar instructional film upheld—superficially—the ideal of education as a leveler of class distinctions, while still emphasizing socio-economic hierarchy as a precondition of literacy.

Reframing does not concern the postwar era only, however, but the present moment in higher education, when colleges and universities are turning to digital technologies to address problems of increasing enrollments, larger class sizes, and other obstacles to access. Ritter argues that the mythological ideal of a one-size-fits-all education that was used to justify the use of instructional films in the 1940s and 50s persists today in the embrace of mass-delivered online literacy instruction, in particular with MOOCs (Massive Open Online Courses). In her analysis, online versions of literacy instruction replicate the postwar instructional film's promise of efficiency and aspiration to erase socioeconomic differences by providing prepackaged, identical instruction to all students, regardless of class or knowledge-based diversity. In doing so these mass-delivered systems, like the instructional film before them, sidestep the agency of teachers to inculcate students in class-based literacies that impede social and economic mobility.

Ritter's first chapter provides the theoretical ground for her argument by surveying a number of scholarly and popular voices, from the postwar era to the present, who demonstrate the prominent role that class-based values have historically played in shaping public education. Stanley Aronowitz, for example, argues that schooling has little impact on students' socioeconomic mobility. Rather, it is the extra-institutional and class-based social networks to which students belong that determine their opportunities for academic and professional achievement. According to Pierre Bourdieu, the role of schools is then to conceal the arbitrary nature of social demarcations under the veil of academic rankings and classifications. Ritter shows how the work of these and other writers who implicate the public schooling system in ideologies of class is supported by ethnographic research illustrating the ways that social stratification plays out in classroom settings. Studies by Jean Anyon, Michael Apple, Harvey Graff, and Shirley Bryce Heath prompt Ritter to ask why, given the abundance of social and economic forces that conspire against upward mobility, the promise of education as a means of transcending one's birth-class continues to hold sway.

In Chapter 2, Ritter proposes that postwar Americans' commitment to the idea of education as a leveling force was motivated not only by the ambition of citizens to succeed in the free market but a civic-minded belief that individual liberation through literacy acquisition would contribute to the country's overall freedom. Ritter shows how this vision, which owed much to the work of John Dewey, was developed by subsequent education theorists in directions that compromised its more progressive aspects. The work of James Bryan Conant in particular upheld Dewey's belief that all students, regardless of socioeconomic background, should have access to quality education. At the same time, he stressed that students' chances of academic success would largely be determined by the social class of their birth. On this view, the path to a "free society" laid in an "informed recognition" of class divisions that made the most of each strata of students' class-based literacies (65). According to Ritter, this modification for a postwar audience of Dewey's notion of education-as-democracy set the philosophical foundation for the postwar instructional film, which was designed to train students to maintain the literacy-based practices of their class rather than provide the tools needed to rise above that class.

In response to curricular proposals like Conant's, educators looked to the instructional film as a method for educating all students, regardless of socioeconomic status or background—without threatening the class structure on which national well-being was felt to depend. It was no accident that these films should appear to educators as the "magic" answer to new demands placed on secondary schools in the postwar era. As Chapter 3 argues, the instructional film industry relied on wide-scale case studies of youth responses to cinema and prevailing pedagogical values to create products that would capture the attention of students while simultaneously strengthening their dependence on class-based literacies. Ritter focuses on the Macmillan Company's twelve volume Payne Fund Studies, which were conducted from 1928–1932 to determine the influence of motion pictures on children's attitudes and behaviors, especially in relation to morality and ethics. Although these studies were motivated by concerns regarding popular cinema's potentially corrupting influence on young viewers, researchers could find no measurable effects of watching films on the attitudes or behaviors of children. According to Ritter, these findings would have supported—paradoxically—the work of the instructional film industry, which deliberately constructed its products *not* to change behavior "but reinforce it, along class lines" (125). She concludes that instructional films were not used to instill new knowledge or behavior in students but to enhance their interest in classroom lessons, which encouraged them to exercise civic responsibility by using the literacies that they already possessed by virtue of their class standing.

Chapters 4 and 5 continue Ritter's account of the instructional film as a mechanism for class maintenance through close readings of films produced by postwar industry leader Coronet Films. The films Ritter analyzes fall into two categories: mental hygiene films that model middle-class attitudes and behaviors and practice-based films that train students in middle-class principles of writing and speaking. Films in the first category depict middle- or upper-class teenagers who learn the social, economic, and/or moral value of attitudes and behaviors appropriate to their social station. The characters who succeed in these lessons are motivated by a desire to maintain their class standing, a concern that is never explicitly discussed but treated as knowledge that viewers share with the persons on-screen. In this way, the films do not provide instruction in the social literacies they depict so much as lessons in who can—and, by implication, who can't—acquire them. More practice-based films by Coronet sought to make the increasingly diverse postwar classroom more manageable terrain for teachers by bringing students' attitudes and behavior into line with middle-class ideals. To that end, the films upheld principles of "good" speaking and writing contemporaneous to their creation, such as accurate retention and clear reporting of information, which encouraged strict adherence to received knowledge. In this way Coronet films did not teach *writing*, which Ritter associates with the creation of new knowledge through invention, but served to reinforce students' commitments to the values and beliefs of their respective social classes.

The final chapter shifts our focus to the present, when colleges and universities are turning to various modes of online instruction to address problems of access to higher education. Her critique focuses primarily on MOOC writing courses, which she regards as inheritors of the instructional film's tendencies to reduce literacy to a set of rote skills and neglect the positionality of users (246). Invoking the work of James Porter, Ritter views MOOCs as "mass instructional products" that replace meaningful teacher-student dialogue with one-way regurgitation of tasks modeled on-screen. In this way, they resemble "a commodity, an object to be bought and sold as if it were a textbook" more than a college course (Porter qtd. in Ritter 261). One consequence of this shift from course to product is a diminishing of the teacher's role: Ritter observes parallels between Denise Comer's remarks on her "elevated and deauthorize[d]" role as instructor in Duke University's MOOC on first-year writing and the way that instructional films demoted teachers from generating course content to mediating prepackaged products (Comer qtd. in Ritter 271). At times, Ritter seems to extend her critique of mass-delivered online instruction to other forms of distance learning, as in her statement that writing is not a "subject to be taught remotely, due to its ideological freight and its basis in individuated instruction" (246). Here, readers invested in online writing instruction may have expected Ritter to address recommendations by scholars in this area for developing online writing courses that are responsive to the needs of nontraditional students. Considered as a whole, however, *Reframing the Subject* should cause us to reevaluate arguments for mass-delivered writing instruction as the answer to problems of educational access in light of past arguments made for technological alternatives to traditional classroom instruction.

The Slow Professor: Challenging the Culture of Speed in the Academy

by Maggie Berg and Barbara K. Seeber
Toronto: U of Toronto Press, 2016. 128 pp.

Reviewed by Sandra D. Shattuck
Pima Community College

As soon as I saw the title of Berg and Seeber's book, I breathed out, as if I were finishing a session of meditation. How wonderful would it be if I could slow my teaching life down? Not obsess over the pile of papers waiting to be responded to and graded. Not worry that my annual self-evaluation would ever get written. To actually read something for pleasure, something that caught my fancy and not something that had to be assessed, deadline attached. What kind of life would that be?

A balanced one. A sane one.

The truth is that many academics in the twenty-first century function on the edge of crazy. But our work-induced desperation is not a topic any of us broaches. Thus, in order to write this book, Berg and Seeber had to push beyond two boundaries: one was the complicit silence muffling the topic, and the other was disciplinary. As Berg and Seeber point out in their introduction, discussing mental health is taboo, even though a large body of research proves that faculty incur increasing stress and work-life imbalance as they take on more and more tasks to fulfill the mandates of the corporate university. Moreover, as Berg and Seeber state, the traditional profile of an academic, which includes "the ideals of mastery, self-sufficient individualism, and rationalism" (12), mitigates against speaking up or collective action. As they state,

> What began simply as helping each other became a sustained investigation of academia. We see our book as uncovering the secret life of the academic, revealing not only her pains but also her pleasures. Writing this book provoked the anxiety of speaking what is habitually left unspoken, and we continually needed to remind ourselves that the oscillation between private shame and the political landscape would prove fruitful. (12)

The corporatization of one's workplace and craft; the loss of health, collegiality, and pleasure in one's work; the increasing isolation of a digitally managed life—these are all big concerns we can discuss in any profession, but Berg and Seeber invite us to focus these concerns on the university. The authors' significant innovation is to apply principles of the Slow movement to academia. In fact, the title of Berg and Seeber's book pays homage to Carl Honoré's seminal text, *In Praise of Slowness: Challenging the Cult of Speed*. But to effect this application, Berg and Seeber had to move beyond their disciplinary boundary as literary critics—they're both professors in departments of English language and literature in Canadian universities—and engage interdisciplinary research and thinking in fields such as psychology, sociology, and management, represented by academic journal titles in the Works Cited pages such as *Journal of Applied Social Psychology*, *Journal of Management Studies*, and *Administrative Science Quarterly*, among others. Offering a succinct assessment of their project and the research required, Berg and Seeber state that "our book is more optimistic than works on the corporate university, more political and historicized than self-help, and more academically focused than those on stress and the Slow movement" (vii).

Stepping out of one's disciplinary comfort zone is no little feat in a business that evaluates its employees on what they know rather on investigating what they don't know. And Berg and Seeber point to this shame and discomfort: "Ironically, our feelings of lack of productivity and not measuring up have not led us until now to 'read' the institution; our self-blame has played into corporate values" (12–13). Their project was not without pushback from colleagues, some of whom told Berg and Seeber "to wake up and get with the program" and that they were "simply too busy to slow down" (11).

Berg and Seeber's diagnosis of the problem in their introduction is well worth the read. "Corporatization" is the villain, and the authors summarize the current literature—a reading list that should be required for all of us who work in academia. Berg and Seeber discuss Benjamin Ginsberg's *The Fall of the Faculty: The Rise of the All-Administrative University and Why It Matters*, and conclude that for universities' strategic plans, "It is the *appearance* of process that counts" (5), not whether or not the plan works. In discussing the increased stress faculty encounter as they collect data and fill in forms, Berg and Seeber cite a useful phrase from Stefan Collini's *What Are Universities For?* Collini's phrase, "fallacy of accountability" (qtd. in Berg and Seeber 5), refers to the idea that as faculty, we are accountable for demonstrating student and course learning outcomes, but that accountability does not ensure that meaningful pedagogical progress occurs.

I am reminded of my own end-of-the-semester housekeeping, when I enter the online halls of data recording by filling in numbers of students who successfully completed an assignment tied to a course learning objective. After I have recorded the number of students who passed or failed the list of assignments, the interface asks me, by pull-down menu, if I want to enter thoughts about how each objective could have been better attained. I decline the invitation. I have already fulfilled the minimum the interface requires of me and after reading and grading hundreds of pages of student writing in the last few weeks of the semester. Moreover, I doubt that the interface will respond to any rushed pedagogical reflection I might offer. I save my thoughts for a private collaborative blog, for small meetings with colleagues, and for the rare professional development opportunity.

This is a small book with a big idea, ninety pages short with four chapters (all under twenty pages each), an introduction and conclusion. Because the book is short does not mean the reader can swallow it in an hour and a half. I found myself stopping often, wondering at epiphanies and further questions. The mostly alliterative chapter titles offer koan-like meditations all by themselves: "Time Management and Timelessness," "Pedagogy and Pleasure," "Research and Understanding," and "Collegiality and Community." The tone is more than collegial—it is friendly and conversational. The book is robustly researched and most sentences offer citations, a practice that initially threw me. I wanted more of the authors' own observations, but I think the pages chock full of research are a reaction to critics who believe Berg and Seeber have stepped too far away from Jane Austen and the Brontës and too close to the self-help aisle. And although the tone is collegial and inviting, Berg and Seeber brook no fools, and that tone can shift into a delightful Austen-esque snarkiness, especially in the chapter on "Time Management and Timelessness," in which texts such as *Graduate Study for the Twenty-First Century* outline twelve-hour days and "Eight Days a Week" (a subheading) as solutions (19). As Berg and Seeber tell academics, "If you are struggling to regain work-life balance, most academic time management literature will not leave you comforted. You may actually feel that you are not working hard enough" (19).

"Time and Timelessness" ends with practical advice: 1) Get off line. 2) Do less. 3) Practice chunks of timeless time. 4) Practice chunks of time doing nothing. 5) Stop talking about time incessantly. Most of us reading these suggestions would shake our heads at the impossibility of such practice, but Berg and Seeber offer enough detail and support that we gain the glimmer of a differently time-ordered working life.

This book is an eminently activist one: Berg and Seeber want us to change the way we work. They understand the Goliath-pressure of corporate education, yet they remain optimistic. So far, I'm with them. However, one area where I wanted more guidance had to do with online education. Berg and Seeber regard online education as anathema to Slow principles and privilege the face-to-face classroom as the only site where we can effectively and affectively resist the culture of speed. The reality of higher education means that courses and entire degree programs are delivered increasingly solely online because online delivery is profitable and fulfills the users' needs to obtain education while working fifty hours a week, being a single parent, and caring for an elderly relative. Despite impossible schedules, students do learn in online environments and instructors do experience some pleasure in their pedagogy (chapter two, "Pedagogy and Pleasure," focuses on this topic). I was disappointed by Berg and Seeber's dismissal of online education and yearned for a robust discussion of Slow principles in this age of MOOCs and five-week accelerated online writing courses offered in the summer.

Another area I wanted Berg and Seeber to address concerns the inequity of faculty labor in universities, which sharply divides the mass of part-time and contingent faculty from full-time and tenure-eligible faculty. The audience for *The Slow Professor* is full-time professors at four-year research institutions (chapter three, "Research and Understanding," focuses solely on that audience), and even though contingent and term-limited faculty and many others can still benefit from much of the advice, the endemic labor injustice of higher education nevertheless imposes a brutal cult of speed for part-timers, whose schedules are marked by rush-hour traffic as they drive from campus to campus.

Although Berg and Seeber do not address online education and labor inequity, their final chapter, "Collegiality and Community," offers a starting place for analysis and action. Indeed, I found some of the most compelling discussion in the authors' description of their collaboration. *The Slow Professor* began as conversation between two English professors about their frustration with ever-increasing administrative paper work in the classroom and diminishing pleasure in their jobs. As they continued to talk and then encountered a national survey on stress conducted by the Canadian Association of University Teachers, Berg and Seeber felt less alone, and their thinking changed: "We shifted our thinking from 'what is wrong with us?' to 'what is wrong with the academic system?'" (2).

"Collegiality and Community" details an increasing "climate of isolation" in the academy, where departmental hallways are emptier and quieter. In their conclusion, Berg and Seeber argue for a simple solution: We need to talk (not text or email) with each other more. And we need to build supportive community through that talking.

Introspection, thinking with others, study, and collaboration all take time—significant and careful time. *The Slow Professor* continues to ask me to reflect on how I mindlessly speed up, as soon as I step into the classroom, and it offers me some guidance on resistance in the last sentence of "The Slow Professor Manifesto": "By taking the time for reflection and dialogue, the Slow Professor takes back the intellectual life of the university" (x).

Composition in the Age of Austerity

Nancy Welch and Tony Scott (Eds.)
Logan: Utah State UP, 2016. 235 pp.

Reviewed by Rachel Buck
University of Arizona

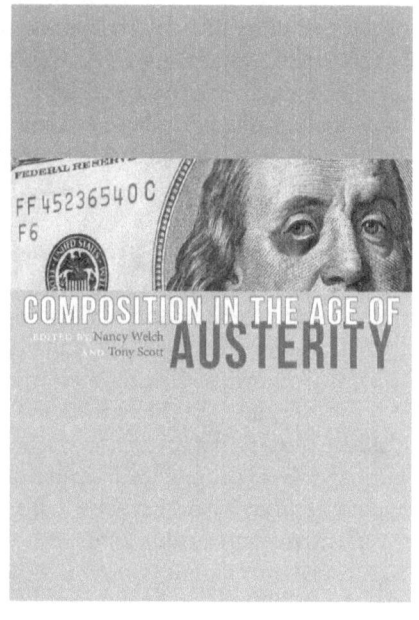

Austerity measures have affected many of us in education and non-profits. Corporate interests have influenced funding opportunities for nonprofits, textbook purchases, assessment issues, curricula, and labor and equity issues. Readers of the *Community Literacy Journal* will be drawn to different sections of this collection, as it is timely and brings together voices to show complex ways that global and national neoliberal formations impact local institutions.

Part I begins with Chris W. Gallagher's discussion of e-portfolios used for accreditation purposes in "Our Trojan Horse: Outcomes Assessment and the Resurrection of Competency-Based Education." Gallagher makes the claim that e-portfolios are part of the neoliberal agenda toward competency-based education (CBE) and that by accepting outcomes assessment, compositionists have "unknowingly invited CBE" (23). Gallagher is critical of private foundations that fund CBE such as the Bill and Linda Gates Foundation, the Lumina Foundation, and Nellie Mae. One of the problems with CBE, as Gallagher states, is that "CBE today imagines writing not as a means of participating in social and civic contexts, but rather as a means of producing material to be evaluated" (29). This is contrasted with how Gallagher imagines writing classes with teachers as "expert shapers of educative experiences . . . who offer a kind and quality of experience—in courses and curricula, and in and through writing—that cannot be replicated or by-passed by vendors" (31). Gallagher ends by giving suggestions for Writing Program Administrators (WPAs) in assisting to get corporate interests out of education reform. Colleges should be places "where people gather to learn together" (32). Gallagher draws a harsh distinction between corporate interests and learning goals, but he does not define what "real" learning might look like or why the two ideas of learning and CBE are mutually exclusive. WPAs are often in a difficult position vying for funding, and may be wary of being called "complicit" in allowing CBE. But there are no quick fixes to educational reforms, and calling on educators and politicians to consider this is an important step.

Deborah Mutnick continues the assessment conversation in Chapter 2: "Confessions of an Assessment Fellow." She is critical of government reform programs such as No Child Left Behind (NCLB) and Obama's Race to the Top and College Scorecard programs. Programs like these have "pitted students and parents against teachers in the name of educational equality and blamed underfunded, high poverty schools, particularly teachers, for academic failure" instead of focusing on fundamental societal issues of racism and poverty (37). For Mutnick, outcomes assessment reduces the "complex process of teaching and learning to a packaged product used to satisfy the promise of excellence, a floating signifier united to any concrete, tangible content, whose meaning we think we know but can never name" (42). As with Gallagher, the term 'learning' is used but not defined contextually. Mutnick claims that many assessments such as standardized tests and rubrics "rarely if at all correlate with what and how students learn" (39). Instead of these assessments, Mutnick would like us to imagine what an assessment would look like that emphasized "students' well-being instead of relying on their performance on tests and rubrics..." (48).

In Chapter 3, Emily J. Isaacs discusses MOOCS (Massive Open Online Courses) in "First-Year Composition Course Redesigns: Pedagogical Innovation or Solution to the 'Cost Disease'?" She analyzes four course redesigns in first-year composition sponsored by Carol Twigg's non-profit National Center for Academic Transformation (NCAT). She admits that Course Redesign as a movement has inspired compositionists' best and worst work—pedagogical work inspired by technological possibilities, but also the work of cost-saving. She concludes through her analysis that redesign efforts include many variables, many of which are often overlooked in assessments, and states, "Beyond an increase in adjuncts and class size, what we see in the 'redesign' of composition is an untheorized and untested return to grammar instruction..." (60).

Marcelle M. Haddix and Brandi Williams end Part I with "Who's Coming to the Composition Classroom?: K-12 Writing In and Outside the Context of Common Core State Standards" in which they compare the writing students are asked to do with CCSS and the writing in a local writing project for urban youth called Writing Our Lives. In their words, the participants in this program get to "interact with the academic writing genres in more authentic ways because they are being asked to produce their own self-sanctioned writing and connect it with their community and events that are important in their lives, as opposed to being assigned a topic by a third party and being asked to write in a manner that may not reflect the student as a writer, but more as a trained student" (69). One of the dangers of the CCSS is that students may think that a form of writing that is not sanctioned by the standards is not considered writing. Their identity as a writer may be formed by these specific standards.

The authors in this section are critical of both private and government funding that is based on outcomes assessments; however, they use undefined terms such as learning, genuine learning, and authentic experiences, but don't unpack those definitions. Their arguments are complicated by their use of undefined terms, but they do bring up challenges about how to assess student learning and the purposes of writing.

Part II moves from funding within the college to funding challenges both inside and outside the college. Each author offers a different perspective and position within their respective organizations and therefore each offers a unique insight into how neoliberal policies impact their material realities and the ideological struggles they face daily. Tom Fox and Elyse Eidman-Aadahl discuss a complicated funding challenge in "The National Writing Project in the Age of Austerity." Based on legislative measures that cut earmarks from the budget in 2011, the NWP's budget went from $25 million to $0 leaving the organization to "reposition itself rhetorically in relation to funding opportunities, emphasizing, for instance, expertise in rural education, science writing, technology, or civic education" (83). Fox and Eidman-Aadahl discuss educator participation in nation-wide conversations, for instance using MOOCS and other maker events that thousands attend, but also discuss how a competition-focused culture creates ideological challenges when applying for grants.

Susan Naomi Bernstein continues this section with "Occupy Basic Writing: Pedagogy in the Wake of Austerity." Because of a lack of funding, many Basic Writing programs have been cut at universities, and with that, many instructors' positions. Bernstein discusses how her own professional identity was closely tied to Basic Writing and the loss of this identity along with programs. Her participation with Occupy Wall Street "offered the material reality of what happens when everyday people not only bear witness to suffering but also work together to attempt to ameliorate suffering" (97). Basic Writing programs are necessary, and she suggests a revised epistemology for Basic Writing based on the material realities of everyday life.

Tobi Jacobi writes "Austerity Behind Bars: The 'Cost' of Prison College Programs" making the claim that until "universities agree to divest corporate ties (to prison profiteers and predatory distance learning programs) and reinvest through committed college programs, the austere life that many experience behind bars and upon reentry will be unlikely to change" (109). Jacobi highlights several prison college programs and literacy initiatives to demonstrate how these programs have responded to the austerity crisis and to show the urgent need for these programs in prisons. Jacobi urges readers to "tactfully resist the urge to serve as pawns—willing or silent—of institutions beguiled by the promise of entrepreneurial survivalism" (116).

In "Buskerfest: The Struggle for Space in Public Rhetorical Education," Mary Ann Cain discusses a service learning course in which she shows students "how public space can level hierarchical social relations and foster creative expression within and between diverse social groups, but also the challenges of partnering with local non-profits that are struggling financially" (121).

Nancy Welch discusses the lack of resources at her institution for the first-year writing program in "First-Year Writing and the Angels of Austerity: A Re-Domesticated Drama." Within neoliberal culture, the "work of education is to be carried out by angels in austerity's architecture, shepherding programs without monetary support and formal workload recognition" (137). Welch worries that this restructuring of first-year composition leads to the "increasingly widespread and naturalized expectation that writing programs can endure without provision, can endlessly adapt to terms of increasingly lean social reproduction" (138).

Many readers will be able to relate in some way to the experiences of the authors in this section, both in writing programs, in local non-profits, and instructors working with students of diverse populations. Each discusses the tensions of working in an environment where the consequences of financial struggles are a reality, but also show that funding is not simply a problem for universities. Neoliberal policies and privatization impact universities, but also the university's ties to public programs. Programs that connect the university with communities allow access to advanced education and address the needs of the public. But many authors also acknowledge the reality of working in a system run by neoliberal policies, and the tension that arises from trying to combat this mentality, while living in the system. There are no easy answers, but Jacobi urges readers to contribute to a "regime of collective care for all people" (117).

Jeanne Gunner opens Part III with ways that those in the system can dissent in "What Happens When Ideological Narratives Lose Their Force?" She begins with strong language for compositionists: "The neoliberal regime has imbued composition theories, pedagogies, and administration, inevitably implicating us all in complicity with corporate values, labor problems, and growing social inequality" (149). But she offers a sort of hope by telling readers that consent as resistance provides a way to fight *against* from *within*. For example, Sid Dobrin's *Postcomposition*, Jeff Rice's *The Rhetoric of Cool*, and the Educ-factory Collective's *Toward a Global Autonomous University*, all find ways to consent while also disrupting by offering alternative ways of thinking and potential new paths. Although Gunner's examples are aimed at a university audience, the idea that consent "can take a creatively disruptive form of complicity, and indirectly consenting to comply with an austerity agenda might open up a space for change" (154) can be a theoretical tool for many institutions and community members who often feel frustrated working *within* austerity measures. This discussion could continue with thoughts of how academics and community literacy practitioners might decide when they can or should *resist* and when they can or should *consent*. This seems a complicated part of Gunner's discussion as conditions will inevitably vary by location, but this approach offers an alternative to hegemonic narratives.

Anne Larson makes the claim in "Composition's Dead" that all levels of education are being "restructured according to capitalism's drive to consolidate power and wealth in the hands of a miniscule percentage of the population at the expense of everyone else" (163). She discusses specifically the labor exploitation in English Departments and questions claims that composition is a living field, claiming, "Composition in particular must stop perceiving itself as having a special, democratic role within the academy. It doesn't" (174). She calls for solidarity, and suggests the "radical step" of focusing energies outside the academy and suggests "collectively withholding teaching and administrative labor, forging coalitions with low-wage workers outside academia, and creating and supporting alternative educational spaces informed by democratic values" (173).

Eileen E. Schell continues the discussion of labor issues and the disparities between higher administration and contingent faculty members in "Austerity, Contingency, and Administrative Bloat: Writing Programs and Universities in an Age of Feast and Famine." She examines the rising administrative costs, precarious faculty ranks, and the rise of student debt. There is an urgency in her conclusion: If we do not have shared governance at our institutions, "we miss the opportunity to preserve what most of believe in despite rank and position: the right of faculty of all ranks to shape higher education curricula and innovative pedagogies and research, the right for higher education instructors to be adequately compensated and fairly treated, and the right for our students to access an affordable, high quality education" (189).

In "Beyond Marketability: Locating Teacher Agency in the Neoliberal University," Shari Stenberg takes up the issue of which teachers count as a "good investment." She discusses various teachers' located agency in repurposing identity categories and shows how embodied locations can be "engaged to challenge, rather than affirm, fixed identity categories" (201).

Tony Scott concludes this section with "Animated by the Entrepreneurial Spirit: Austerity, Dispossession, and Composition's Last Living Act." In this chapter, Scott criticizes the 2015 Conference on College Composition and Communication (CCCC) conference call and theme of "Risk and Reward." The conference call is one way that the spirit of entrepreneurialism contributes to the "field's dissolution and full absorption into the 'free' market" (207). This "entrepreneurial turn" in academia includes tuition hikes, textbook company partnerships, curricular technologies, food service contractors, sports apparel companies, and other university schemes.

This collection is in no way exhaustive of the many issues that colleges and universities are facing, but it is a useful starting point in many ways. Economic problems exist on global, national, and local levels, but the way they impact local institutions varies. This collection offers insights for university educators and administrators, WPAs, and non-profit organizations, many of whom are in uniquely difficult decision-making positions. One notable absence in the collection was the mention of increasing numbers of international students at US institutions, many of whom pay full tuition and receive no financial aid. Although many of these issues are local and colleges and universities might discuss them differently, this collection offers valuable insight with regard to growing concerns that affect the material realities of faculty, students, non-profit staff, and administrators, much of which will resonate with *Community Literacy Journal* readers.

Grassroots Literacies:
Lesbian and Gay Activism and the Internet in Turkey

Serkan Görkemli
New York: SUNY Press, 2014. 233 pp.

Reviewed by Madelyn Pawlowski
University of Arizona

Few studies in rhetoric and composition have explored the bridge between literacy and the study of sexuality beyond the context of the U.S. writing classroom. Thus, Serkan Görkemli's *Grassroots Literacies: Lesbian and Gay Activism and the Internet in Turkey* has been recognized as a major contribution to the field because of connections it makes between literacy and transnational discourses of sexuality and gender. Through engaging interviews, textual analyses, and historical insights, Görkemli proposes a "literacy-based approach to studying transnational rhetorics of sexuality in cross-cultural and international LBGT communities" (19). Recognized by the Conference on College Composition and Communication as the winner of the 2015 Lavender Rhetorics Award for Excellence in Queer Scholarship, Görkemli's analysis of Legato, an Internet-based LGBT collegiate student group in Turkey, is potentially influential for scholars of community literacy, queer rhetorics, new media, and transnational feminism.

As explained in Chapter 1, Görkemli theorizes Legato's grassroots activism using the concepts of "sexual literacy," "community literacy," and "sponsors of literacy" while also addressing literacy as a societal force and an "individual resource or practice" (19). Through this literacy-based analysis, Görkemli investigates the "individual and collective rhetorical agency and power (or lack thereof) that are necessary to generate, disseminate, and, at times, oppose representations of homosexuality in culturally and geographically diverse contexts" (12). The book immerses readers in Turkey's mid-1990s LGBT activist scene. Legato, the main organization under analysis, was founded in 1996 in an effort to initiate activism on college campuses. What began as a group of students organizing social activities such as film screenings and discussion groups at Middle East Technical University quickly spread to online spaces and college campuses throughout Turkey. By December of

2000, there were 27 Legato groups at 27 universities. In just three years, the numbers grew to 857 members at 83 colleges and universities. Unifying these individual factions and contributing to the group's accelerated growth was a shared *Yahoo!* group mailing list and the establishment of a Legato website. Through their hybrid presence, Legato groups disseminated sexual literacy, particularly in regards to Euro-American discourses of sexuality and LGBT identities, as well as language and tools to "critique heterosexism, the social institutions that uphold it, and the underlying biological views of gender and sexuality" (17). Their actions depended on the digital literacy of their members and community literacy, or rather, a search for alternative discourses through action, reflection, and collective action. Legato took on the role of a "sponsoring institution," in that it supported members in linking their personal sexuality with a community seeking public recognition and rights. Other competing sponsors of literacy for Legato members included the non-collegiate LGBT advocacy organization known as Kaos GL (Kaos Gay and Lesbian Cultural Research and Solidarity Association), popular media, and the nationalist state. Later chapters further explore these competing influences on Legato members.

Chapter 2 introduces readers to the dominant rhetorics of homosexuality in Turkey including the popular understanding of homosexuality as "sexual inversion," the assumption that homosexuals desire to adopt the behaviors of the opposite gender. Two Turkish celebrities serve as examples of how mass media reinforced this rhetoric of sexual inversion: Zeki Müren, a queer male singer "who wore makeup and women's clothing," and Bülent Ersoy, a "male-to-female transsexual singer" (39). While on the surface, these individuals transgressed gender norms, neither individual publicly identified as LGBT or queer and their success depended on a bargain with heterosexual normativity. Lesbianism was left largely unacknowledged in mass media even into the 2000s, and widespread oppression of the *travestiler,* the everyday self-identified queer subject in Turkey, was commonplace. Viewed as socially deviant men and often assumed to be sex workers, *travesti* were subject to police violence and familial and societal discrimination. In order to combat these sensationalized, simplistic, and negative representations of homosexuality, Legato members made flyers portraying male and female homosexuals to advertise their campus events and distributed a zine with definitions of "homosexuality" and "lesbian" along with erotic art. Görkemli analyzes the visual rhetoric of flyers, zines, and the Legato website in order to demonstrate how Legato helped introduce "a new visual vocabulary and literacy that defied the rhetorics of homosexuality as sexual inversion," and provided Legato's young adult population "with critical tools to test its rhetorical agency and power" (60). This chapter sets up the rhetorical situation for readers, setting the stage for the next chapter, the heart of the book containing Görkemli's analysis of five narratives from Legato members concerning their sexual literacy.

Though the third chapter is called "Coming Out," Görkemli challenges both the genre of the coming out narrative and the literacy narrative, which have been critiqued as simplistic, linear, and utopian. Legato members' experiences "confirm that coming out does not necessarily follow the normative narrative arc of complete emancipation" (120). Some of the individuals interviewed never came out to their families, for example. In his "interpretive portraitures" of the participants, Görkemli first reports participant interviews with extensive quotes, attempting to amplify participant voices before inserting his interpretive gaze. Through this thoughtful organizational structure, he constructs a complex view of the multiple gateways and sponsors of both heterosexual and LGBT literacies that complicated Legato members' attempts to come out in Turkish society.

The narratives provide evidence that television and the Internet served as gateways to LGBT literacies. In addition—or rather in opposition—to Müren and Ersoy, the participants referenced gay characters from American television shows such as *Real World* and *Melrose Place* as early influences on their sexual literacy. Seeing masculine gay men and evidence of lesbianism and bisexualism on TV confirmed "there are different ways of being a homosexual" (103). Through other gateways such as Internet search engines and online chat rooms, participants located communities of homosexual Turks, leading to involvement in Legato and Kaos GL. As a sponsor of sexual literacy, Legato introduced the participants to social constructionist discourses of sexuality. Before joining Legato, as one of the participants explains, "I didn't have anything to do with or any knowledge about social issues . . . [or] minorities . . . Legato pushed my perspective on homosexuality ten years forward" (105). Legato members served as sponsors for each other as they shared their experiences, research findings, and perspectives online and across college campuses. Families and schools provided participants with access to computers and the English language, which opened opportunities for exploring human rights developments and LGBT issues happening abroad.

However, families and educational institutions also served as gateways and sponsors of heterosexual literacy. Participant experiences provide evidence of prevailing familial homophobia driven by religious and political rhetoric that characterized homosexuality as deviant, perverse, and punishable. Though homosexuality has never been explicitly illegal in Turkey, "participants grew up watching televised police violence toward non-gender-conforming *travesti* citizens on television" (107). Educational institutions also played a significant role in sponsoring heterosexual literacy; most participants did not take any courses that covered sexuality until college, as the subject was seen as "taboo" and an illegitimate area of study. In drawing attention to the multiple sponsors of both LGBT and heterosexual literacy in the participant narratives, Görkemli demonstrates the coming out process as a complex sexual literacy event composed of multiple literacy practices. The narratives are powerfully presented and carefully analyzed, leaving readers with a greater understanding not just of Turkish society and LGBT activism, but how to conduct a transnational analysis of sexual literacy that acknowledges the complexity of participants' experiences without submitting entirely to conventions of the coming out or literacy narrative genres.

Chapter 4 delves deeper into how Legato's uses of digital media both aided and undermined the group's activist efforts. Görkemli returns to three of the participant narratives to trace their digital and non-digital involvement with Legato and other related LGBT activist groups. Their experiences show the contradicting benefits and drawbacks of computer-mediated activity; on the one hand, websites, mailing lists, and chat rooms helped broaden Legato's influence and provided an opportunity for individuals to anonymously participate in conversations about LGBT identities and culture, while on the other hand, participants abandoned offline efforts to make their presence known on college campuses, leading to what one Legato member describes as "talk without any result" (157). In short, a lack of continuity grew between the online and offline incarnations of Legato, leading activist leaders to issue calls for participants to "come out" of their "digital closets." Görkemli explains how the tensions between the digital and non-digital practices of Legato played a role in the group's eventual demise and calls on community activists to pay attention to how digital media can work for or against the building of sustainable community literacy efforts. Though Legato is no longer active, readers will find Görkemli's analysis of their early successes and failures at using digital media reminiscent of current debates regarding the effectiveness of online activism, sometimes referred to as "slacktivism" (e.g. changing one's Facebook profile picture or using hashtags to show support of a social issue, signing online petitions, or re-tweeting political messages).

The author concludes with a request for similar literacy-based analyses of sexuality in international contexts. Görkemli urges other scholars to account for multiple influences on sexual literacy, as is demonstrated through his analysis of the role of media (print, television, and the Internet) and discourses of religion, heterosexuality, and nationalism. Görkemli's intricate weaving of participant voices with visual rhetorical analysis, historical and cultural insights, and key concepts from literacy studies is the overall strength of this book. Indeed, it sets a precedent for future transnational studies of sexuality and international grassroots movements.

The Desire for Literacy: Writing in the Lives of Adult Learners

Lauren Rosenberg
Urbana: CCCC/NCTE Studies in Writing and Rhetoric (SWR) series, 2015. 185 pp.

Reviewed by Sally Benson
University of Arizona

What does literacy mean, and why does it matter? Lauren Rosenberg posits that literacy, a term that remains contested, is not merely a set of skills but "a means of knowing and interacting in the world that can be shared" (154). Rosenberg's book is the result of a qualitative study about adult literacy learners' writing practices and their reasons for seeking literacy skills. Referring to Gayatri Chakravorty Spivak's *subaltern class*, "that sector of the population whose experience counters the dominant and who are, therefore, shut out from dominant ideological concerns" (3), Rosenberg raises the question of whether those who have been positioned by dominant literate discourses as voiceless and without knowledge can gain the tools not only to be heard and to exercise their voices, but also to challenge the scripts that have been ascribed to them. Observing students at Read/Write/Now Adult Learning Center in Springfield, Massachusetts, Rosenberg focuses her study on four older adults, George, Violeta, Chief, and Lee Ann (pseudonyms), who are no longer in the workforce and who have voluntarily chosen to become literacy learners. She invites us to ask the important question: What are the motivations of these individuals, who have been rendered mute by societal values that equate literacy with intelligence, to become more literate?

Rosenberg offers intimate accounts of these older adults and places them in the role of being teachers, carefully attentive to her own role as researcher and as representative of dominant literate culture. Relating to her participants as a learner, Rosenberg aims to hear their stories without assumptions. While collaborating with her participants, Rosenberg successfully demonstrates a model of creating a space in which both researcher and subject are interchangeable roles. She also sets an example of how theories are formed and articulated, and of how we might reconsider where we place credit for such scholarship. Through careful listening, she seeks to hear how the participants of her study theorize their roles as "nonliterates" and how they describe their experiences of and purposes for seeking literacy education. Rosenberg's research gives voice to those traditionally ignored. Through this approach, these individuals become literacy theorists and help make a methodological contribution to literacy studies.

Rosenberg's primary methodology is narrative inquiry. She uses interviews to explore the relationship between the written and spoken stories of her participants. As they reframe and retell their spoken narratives in their writing, Rosenberg observes how they restore or "restory" themselves in a dominant position of knowing. As these four participants talk about their experiences around literacy, all are aware that they have been positioned as being voiceless and unknowing people. Carefully avoiding power dynamics of researcher and subject, Rosenberg maintains casual relationships with her participants. "What started out as a research study ended up as an engaged conversation" for Rosenberg, who is invested in hearing their stories (21). By sharing their personal stories with her, and by restorying themselves through their writing, these participants place their reasons for becoming literate in direct opposition to a culture that has marginalized them. In spite of their lack of tradition literacy skills, they are adults who have led rich lives full of experiences and who are, in fact, knowledgeable.

In Chapter 1, "Resisting Nonliteracy: Adult Learners Restory Their Narratives," we meet George, an African American man in his sixties learning literacy skills. Rosenberg echoes the Freirean belief that education should be designed by the people based on their own experiences as thinkers rather than imposed on them as a social weapon. She places George in a position of co-author, illustrating that the adult literacy learner participants of the study are ideally suited to teach those concerned with community literacy studies. George knows what it feels like to be embarrassed as nonliterate, and he reaches out to help a woman read a sign in a way that doesn't inflict the same embarrassment on her. In telling his narrative, George empowers himself through the role of knower. As adult learners develop literacy skills, they both accept and resist dominant discourses of literacy, according to Rosenberg, as they straddle their roles of being subjected *to* this ideology as well as being subjects *of* it. They want acceptance in the literate mainstream, but they also resist the unjust practices that have been used to marginalize them.

Chapter 2, "Speaking from 'the Silent, Silenced Center': 'Just Because You Can't Read Doesn't Mean That You Don't Know'" describes the participants' experiences of nonliteracy. Rosenberg points to Krista Ratcliffe's insistence on researchers not just listening closely to participants but listening differently to them. Ratcliffe upends the word "understanding" to become "standing under" and suggests standing under the discourses of people talking about themselves as a means of becoming informed by them (26). Rosenberg chooses to *stand under* the words of her participants' stories, listening without judgment and allowing their words to wash over her and over us as readers.

In Chapter 2, we meet Rosenberg's four participants, all of whom share a common experience of not having had consistent access to school. We are first introduced to Violeta, who grew up in Puerto Rico and New York City. Violeta's parents, resistant to her being in school, moved back and forth between Puerto Rico and New York, challenging Violeta as a learner. We then learn about Chief, who was raised on a sharecropper's farm in the pre-Civil Rights South, and Chief's access to schooling revolved around seasons, weather, and fighting between whites and blacks. Despite his lack of formal education, Chief led a reasonably mainstream life as a welder and forklift operator. Next, we meet Lee Ann, raised by a nonliterate mother who refused to buy her the books she desired as a child and who moved the family frequently to avoid rent collectors. We also discover that George, like Chief, was raised on a sharecropper's farm and did not attend school regularly. He had a career as a metal forger and later as a machine operator and successfully hid his nonliteracy behind competent job performance.

Rosenberg ends Chapter 2 by calling into question her role as a listener. Lee Ann shares an experience of being kicked out of her church choir for not being able to read music or lyrics. She tells her story of being belittled by the choir director, "he crushed me like a bug . . . " (47), and she places responsibility on the listener, and now on us as readers, to acknowledge the ways mainstream literacy can be used as a weapon to marginalize alternative forms of literacy.

Chapter 3, "Contemplating Literacy: 'A Door Now Open'" takes us inside Read/Write/Now, which places student writing at the center of its curriculum. Instructors at R/W/N observe that adult learners, unlike most children, voluntarily invest in their own learning. Rosenberg's participants contemplate literacy as a process of *becoming*, and Rosenberg describes them as literacy researchers (57). Both Violeta and Lee Ann experience literacy skills as a means to become more independent, less reliant upon others. As a form of self-reflection, Chief writes letters to himself acknowledging his progress and expressing his pride in that growth. He nurtures himself in ways he did not receive nurturing as a child. He wants to circulate his writing for others to be inspired to pursue learning. George is protective of his status as learner. He places pride in working and in the self-sufficiency it afforded him. He chooses to learn to read and write because of the freedom it allows him. Through reading, for example, he can learn about China, a location that would have remained a mystery without literacy.

In Chapter 4, "Literacy and Nonliteracy: Reflective Knowledge and Critical Consciousness," the participants describe literacy as a form of power in contrast to their experience of nonliteracy. By learning to write, Lee Ann is discovering herself and is able to empathize with other struggling students at Read/Write/Now, which leads to her self-validation. George understands power relationships because of his metal work at the drop forge, and he is able to theorize about those who use their literacy as a means to subjugate and control others. George's earlier narrative about helping a woman who cannot read illustrates his experience as both nonliterate/Other and as literate mentor. He recognizes ways in which literacy can be used to demean or denigrate people, and he intervenes to help a woman read a sign in a store. Violeta uses her literacy to move away from a position of being oppressed to a position of control and independence. Chief sees literacy skills as educational skills, and he likes to share his knowledge to inspire others to study. All have used their access to literacy as a tool for empowerment and liberation. By theorizing about literacy through the telling of their own experiences, and through their criticism of the conditions of their nonliteracy, these four participants teach us that literacy and educational access are tools of social violence and segregation. Their accounts of writing as a form of resistance illustrate Freire's perspective on becoming literate as a means of decolonization or of countering their subjugation.

In Chapter 5, "What Writing Enables," Rosenberg describes the relationship to writing that Violeta and Chief have as form of textual agency. Their increased confidence in writing allows them to voice their opinions and to reach out to others as a form of social transformation. Violeta, hoping to inspire others to take control over their lives, positions herself as a voice against poverty and nonliteracy and eventually participates in educating the Latino community about HIV. For Chief, literacy is a form of self-validation. Chief positions himself in the role of educator by distributing his stories of being nonliterate and of being racially discriminated against at school in his church's newsletter. Writing validates his opinions by documenting his words, making them permanent. In other words, Chief writes to *be* himself. Both Violeta and Chief use writing as a tool for personal realization and as a form of social action. As they demonstrate their success to others, Violeta and Chief reposition themselves as advocates against social, political, and economic Othering. They "consciously subvert the culture that has oppressed them when they write" (144).

The final chapter, "The Transgressive Power of Writing," begins with a quote from Chief, "[A] lot of stuff down there was kept hush-mouth" (146). Chief's experience of growing up in the segregated South taught him that not being able to read or write meant not having a voice. The dominant culture of mainstream literacy casts a societal muzzle on nonliterates, rendering them "hush-mouth" or silenced. Rosenberg's four authors reject their position as nonliterate subjects through their desire for literacy, and this desire to undo their subjugation is a resistance to being Othered. Their desire and success to be literate directly challenges identities society has imposed upon them and which they had previously absorbed. In fact, they labor to reposition themselves as liberated. Through these stories, Rosenberg shows that in order to disrupt the label of Other, one must first become self-aware and aware of the *desire* for literacy.

Desire for literacy, writes Rosenberg, is not the same as need for literacy. According to Rosenberg, the fields of writing studies and of adult basic education (ABE) do not focus enough on why people desire literacy, nor do they focus exclusively on adult learners. Research in writing studies most often fixates on college students, and scholarship in ABE emphasizes reading practices and the functional uses of writing (155). Writing, as textual agency, is at the core of Rosenberg's study on adult literacy. As the four participants shift from nonliterate to literate, their purposes for writing evolve. Writing moves beyond being a form of self-discovery and of restorying their own identities to a tool for social action and for leveraging others. Their writing becomes an act of resistance against oppression, and their interaction with it is constantly changing.

Lauren Rosenberg addresses an important and overlooked population of learners of literacy—older adults who seek literacy skills later in life. Specifically, she explores the *why*. The reasons people remain nonliterate and don't get the schooling needed to be literate adults remain understudied, and Rosenberg addresses these essential points. She shows us the power of writing as an act of transgression by her participants and acknowledges these authors as teachers, reminding us that marginalized individuals have much to teach us about perspectives of subordination and, in this context, of the violence of literacy. Her participants' narratives emerge as multi-dimensional theories about literacy and extend beyond flatter theories of nonliterates as merely learners. As Rosenberg gets to know George, Violeta, Chief, and Lee Ann and follows their respective journeys to becoming literate, she re-thinks what literacy means as she tries to understand how these four adults define it. As we readers *stand under* her co-authors' words and stories, we enter spaces where literacy reaches beyond academic purposes.

Rosenberg leaves us with a sense that literacy means faith, knowledge, decolonization, independence, pleasure, social action, validation, representation, empowerment, and much more. Literacy learning, writes Rosenberg, "takes a person, the learners along with their teachers—to remote parts of the mind and soul that we might not know exist, those places of wandering and rumination that involve the reliving aspects of reading and writing, taking it in and traveling there again" (155). Anyone who is invested in adult literacy for communities outside of traditional education, and in shifting the imbalance of cultural capital that literacy often represents, should read Rosenberg's book. Her participants, whose perspectives extend beyond those representative of a dominant discourse, have much to teach us about the multifaceted role that literacy has in our lives. Voices of these historically silenced individuals surface as voices of knowledgeable theorists thanks to Rosenberg's important research.

Freedom Writing:
African American Civil Rights Literacy Activism, 1955–1967

Rhea Estelle Lathan
Urbana: CCCC/NCTE Studies in Writing and Rhetoric (SWR) series, 2015. 143 pp.

Reviewed by Eric A. House
University of Arizona

Freedom Writing: African American Civil Rights Literacy Activism by Rhea Estelle Lathan rests on the intersections of the African American rhetorical tradition and community literacy. This project introduces the term "gospel literacy" to illustrate the complex and innovative literacy practices of the Sea Island Citizenship School teachers and participants from the Civil Rights era. Activism is also in the forefront of the discussion, as the histories and narratives of the Citizenship School suggest a literacy practice that moves beyond reading and writing skills and into discussions of critical consciousness and civic freedom. Lathan is explicit in naming literacy within a social constructivist paradigm, and aligns her work with that of social historians who attempt to examine the ideological and functional relationships between literacy and broader political ideals (xxiii). *Freedom Writing* is a moment of recovery as Lathan urges readers to follow her on an exploration of the Citizenship School for an innovative perspective on literacy, of which will come a revised vocabulary for discussing the literacy histories of marginalized groups (xiii).

Chapter one begins the act of recovery by first tracing the histories of her main term "gospel literacy." Lathan starts with a brief history of gospel, tracing the term back to Thomas Dorsey in 1932 who coined it as a music genre. Gospel music extended beyond Negro spirituals because of its inclusion of secular rhythms with spiritual lyrics, while Negro spirituals were primarily in a European musical style pushed onto African American people. They also differed in that spirituals "rested on a fantasy of hoping for a better life in the hereafter, but gospel held tight to the promise of a better life right now" (1).

Lathan then moves into a working definition of gospel literacy, starting first by naming and explaining four fundamental components of gospel consciousness: call-

and response, acknowledging the burden, bearing witness, and finding redemption. "Call-and-response" might be thought of as an expression of both ritualized communal unity and a spontaneous expression of individual freedom (9). It is a way of knowing, and it makes literacy participatory and not something to be observed from afar (10). "Acknowledging the burden" relies on the conviction that history and power are synonymous. Understanding this component as foundational to gospel literacy is essential as it represents a moving past suffering and despair through demonstrating how history changes when people take authority over their literacy practices (18). The meaning of "bearing witness" draws from Geneva Smitherman's definition of testifying, as Lathan quotes Smitherman's description as "a ritualized form of black communication in which the speaker gives verbal witness to the efficacy, truth and power of some experience in which all blacks have shared" (18). Lathan hails bearing witness as foundational to gospel literacy, since her goal is to seek a definition of literacy that exists at the intersections of the individual and the community. Bearing witness accomplishes this by communicating life-giving or life-changing experiences and relating them to larger social systems.

The fourth component, finding redemption, illustrates the importance of recovery in Lathan's project. Drawing on Zora Neale Hurston, Lathan claims that the concepts of understanding and interpreting histories provide moments to consider theoretical intellectualisms that intersect with African American cultural norms (23). Finding redemption is then pivotal to the project, as it demonstrates, "a means of explaining how deep cultural resources that develop in the church and spiritual life transfer to a secular context as intellectual and spiritual strategies that enhance literacy activism," all of which, in this instance, might be done through a recovery of the Citizenship School narrative (24). The strength in chapter one lies in Lathan's framing of gospel literacy, but it isn't until the subsequent chapters that readers witness the complexity of the frame when told through the Citizenship School narrative.

Chapter two begins the exploration of gospel literacy as seen in the Citizenship School narrative through the gospel component of acknowledging the burden. The burden in this instance had to do with the issues presented to African Americans in the Reconstruction era as they fought state mandates that utilized literacy as a tool to exclude blacks from voting, which would then exclude them from shaping the political atmosphere of the communities they inhabited. Lathan maps the history of the Citizenship School that arose in the Sea Islands of South Carolina, claiming that participation in these schools were "fueled by the failed attempts of the local and federal governments to sponsor adult literacy initiatives for African Americans" (38). The success of the Sea Island Citizenship School might be attributed to an ability to acknowledge and understand the areas where past practices failed. Lathan also attributes it to the adoption of a philosophy that believes in the dignity, knowledge, intellectual competence, and capacity for growth possessed by adult learners despite their level of reading, writing, or other academic experience (39).

Call-and-response takes center stage in chapter three, as Lathan utilizes it to illustrate and theorize communal performances that were on the intersections of literacy acquisition and civic freedom. She begins with the call, marking it as the moment when Citizenship School teachers and learners Esau Jenkins, Bernice Robinson, and Septima Clark attended a workshop that sought to create solidarity between African American social justice crusades and global social justice movements. The end of the workshop involved a series of questions (the call) that asked participants, "What are we going to do when we get back home? How are we going to transmit our experiences this week back in our community?" (44). Esau Jenkins responded with a call of his own that emphasized high levels of illiteracy in his community, all of which had a negative impact on voter registration. It is out of Jenkins's call that the instantiation of the Citizenship Schools would occur.

As Jenkins, Robinson, and Clark began their literacy work with the participants in the Sea Island Citizenship School, the need grew for something deeper than just literacy gains for the sake of voter registration. Lathan notes this as she quotes Bernice Robinson, who stated,

> ...we accepted the black school, we accepted the whites and the colored fountain as a way of life. I knew that there was a lot illiteracy around me, but I accepted that as a fact, that there was nothing you could do about it.... When Esau started talking about it, then, you know, it started to really coming through and something to think about. People can't read, you know. So he turned a whole workshop around; [laughs] everybody became interested in this, you know? (51)

Robinson's words resonated with various experiences of the participants in the Citizenship School, with some connecting more with the sovereign freedom they gained through literacy acquisition (66). Lathan acknowledges the necessity for such a variety in her theorizing, stating, "call-and-response is a process that acknowledges diverse voices and diverse experiences, including the meaning(s) of civic freedom, within participants' teaching and learning activities" (66).

In chapter four, Lathan looks at the curriculum as well as the interactions within the Citizenship School classes, using the component of "bearing witness" as a lens. Lathan's argument that gospel literacy rests at the intersection of both literacy acquisition and social activism continues in this chapter. She notes that the Citizenship School curriculum required learners to not only become aware of the problems in their world and the worlds of others, but also to begin asking questions and proposing solutions (78). Lathan brings in Paulo Freire's framing of critical consciousness in *Pedagogy of the Oppressed* to aid in making sense of the class and curriculum experiences of the Citizenship School. One explicit connection occurs in the teachers' desire to not be seen as expert in the eyes of students, illustrated when Lathan quotes an unidentified teacher, stating, "I tell people, I'm not Jesus Christ. I didn't die on the cross for you. I cannot carry you over to Canaan. You have to walk over there for yourself" (89). Such a statement brings up Freire's conception of co-intentionality as a key factor in a liberating education, as it suggests that students must claim agency *with* their teachers and be recognized as Subjects that can both critically know their realities and take ownership of their knowledges (Freire 69).

Lathan ends chapter four by analyzing a class interaction that demonstrates how a class focused on completing a voter registration application transitioned into a means of testifying and sharing ways of knowing (96). The interaction between the students and instructor show various instances of students questioning language that traditionally disenfranchised African American people, one example being *pardoned* as a term that carried significant social and political implications (103). Lathan notes that participants in those moments don't accept quick definitions of terms. Instead, they wish to discuss what it means on various levels, from them, to the registrar, to the State of South Carolina (103–4). The final chapter focuses on the example of Bernice Robinson as a model for the fifth component, finding redemption. In further defining this fifth component, Lathan states that finding redemption is the overarching theme of gospel literacy as it is a theoretical interpretive concept that disrupts the myth that names grassroots literacy acquisition and use as basic, simple, or mechanical (106). The history of Bernice Robinson and her work with the Citizenship School are a paradigm of gospel literacy, as her narrative illustrates a moment where an intense spiritual and cultural way of being worked as literacy activism in a political context (107).

Lathan claims that Bernice Robinson engaged in a "finding redemption" ideology by insisting on having a place in the history of the Citizenship Schools (107). While Robinson's role in literacy acquisition among African Americans in the civil rights era has been historically diminished, her participation in interviews in the late 1970s (as well as her story recounted by Lathan) illustrate the ability for memory to be critical part to redemption. Lathan claims that memory itself can be considered composition, as we continually revise our memories, rewriting them into stories that bring understanding (109).

The place of redemption and recovery in Lathan's conception of gospel literacy not only provides an overarching theme, but also provides readers with a call that is best communicated with Lathan's own words:

> My efforts of recovery through this book are aimed toward one goal: if I can link the grassroots literacy activities of African American Civil Rights Movement to contemporary literacy issues, then many troubled students in community literacy programs, especially black women who are otherwise at risk for harmful activities, might identify with these ordinary grassroots heroines and focus their energies in a creative direction. (112)

Lathan's attempt to recover the narratives of historically marginalized grassroots literacy activists speaks to the necessity for a continued recovery of similar histories as well as the continued connection of such histories to contemporary issues. Such connections create possibilities for others to continue the work of literacy activism that will be necessary in impacting our respective communities during this time of political division and uncertainty. Possibly best suited for those readers with an interest in adult education as well as those involved with grassroots community programs, the histories of literacy activists like Bernice Robinson reminds scholars, teachers, and students alike that community literacy work can recognize and recover the literacy histories of marginalized groups. These histories also ask that we remember the spiritual components of literacy in addition to the alphanumeric.

Works Cited

Freire, Paulo. *Pedagogy of the Oppressed*. Trans. Myra Berman Ramos. New York: Continuum, 1990. Print.

DEPARTMENT OF
WRITING, RHETORIC, & DISCOURSE

Master of Arts Degrees in
NEW MEDIA STUDIES
WRITING, RHETORIC, & DISCOURSE
with concentrations in
Professional & Technical Writing
Teaching Writing & Language

Graduate certificate in TESOL
Combined BA/MA in WRD

Bachelor of Arts in WRITING, RHETORIC, & DISCOURSE
Minor in **Professional Writing**

 facebook.com/DePaulWRD   @DePaulWRD

WRD.DEPAUL.EDU

Congratulations to These Award Winners & WPA Scholars!

Antiracist Writing Assessment Ecologies: Teaching and Assessing Writing for a Socially Just Future by Asao Inoue
   Best Book Award, CCCC (2017)

The WPA Outcomes Statement—A Decade Later
   Edited by Nicholas N. Behm, Gregory R. Glau, Deborah H. Holdstein, Duane Roen, and Edward M. White
   Best Book Award, Council of Writing Program Adminstrators (July, 2015)

GenAdmin: Theorizing WPA Identities in the Twenty-First Century by Colin Charlton, Jonikka Charlton, Tarez Samra Graban, Kathleen J. Ryan, & Amy Ferdinandt Stolley
   Best Book Award, Council of Writing Program Adminstrators (July, 2014)

Mics, Cameras, Symbolic Action: Audio-Visual Rhetoric for Writing Teachers by Bump Halbritter
   Distinguished Book Award, *Computers and Composition* (May, 2014)

New Releases

The Framework for Success in Postsecondary Writing: Scholarship and Applications edited by Nicholas N. Behm, Sherry Rankins-Robertson, and Duane Roen

Labored: The State(ment) and Future of Work in Composition edited by Randall McClure, Dayna V. Goldstein, and Michael A. Pemberton

Oral Communication in the Disciplines: A Resource for Teacher Development and Training by Deanna P. Dannels, Patricia R. Palmerton, & Amy L. Housley Gaffney

www.parlorpress.com

www.ingramcontent.com/pod-product-compliance
Lightning Source LLC
Chambersburg PA
CBHW031600170426
43196CB00032B/929